THE 4 SPIRITUAL LAWS OF MONEY

THE
4 SPIRITUAL
LAWS OF
MONEY

YOUR JOURNEY *to* **REAL WEALTH**

JULIE MARIE MURPHY,
CLU, CHFC, MBA, CFP®

BEYOND YOUR WILDEST DREAMS, LLC
CHICAGO

THE 4 SPIRITUAL LAWS OF MONEY

YOUR JOURNEY *to* REAL WEALTH

© 2022 Julie Marie Murphy, CFP®

ISBN: 978-0-9801133-3-4 paperback
ISBN-978-0-9801133-4-1 eBook
Library of Congress Control Number: 2022917100

Cover Design by:
Molly Reeser, MACook Design

Printed in the United States of America

PLEASE NOTE: The views, comments, and opinions expressed within this writing are solely those of Julie Murphy, not those of any co-workers, managers, broker-dealer staff or management, regulators, or other industry professionals, except where specifically cited. The ideas and opinions presented are not meant to fit every individual, and, in some cases, professional help, in the form of medical, tax, and legal advice, may be necessary and should be obtained from qualified professionals before attempting to implement serious changes in your life.

The hypothetical situations discussed in this book are based on real life examples. Names and circumstances have been changed. The opinions voiced in this material are for general information only and are not intended to provide specific advice or recommendations for any individual. To determine which investments or strategies may be appropriate for you, consult your financial advisor prior to investing.

Julie Murphy does not offer tax advice. The tax information contained herein is general and not exhaustive by nature. It was not intended or written to be used—and cannot be used—by any taxpayer for the purpose of avoiding penalties that may be imposed under US federal tax laws. Federal and state tax laws are complex and constantly changing. You should always consult your own legal or tax advisor for information concerning your individual situation.

This material is neither an offer to sell nor the solicitation of an offer to buy any security, which can only be made by the prospectus, which has been filed or registered with the appropriate state and federal agencies, and sold only by the broker/dealers authorized to do so. No regulatory agency has passed on or endorsed the merits of this material. Any representations to the contrary are unlawful. All trademarks or copyrights referenced herein are the property of their respective owners.

— writes from the
perspective of victims
of circumstances; and the
is the audience she
attracts.

What are *The 4 Spiritual Laws of Money*™?

Manifestation Begins with Desire

The Heart is Stronger Than the Brain

Intention Redirects Energy

The Universe Responds to Action

DEDICATION

I dedicate this book to my mom,
Mary Adele Erxleben Murphy

MY MOM, MARY Murphy, is a devout Catholic, but her spiritual gifts go way deeper than going to church on Sundays. The greatest gift she ever gave me, my siblings, and all others who crossed her path was the gift of holding a safe space for us to grow into the human beings we came here to be. She always held that space of neutrality, absent of any blame, shame, guilt, or judgment. That space allowed the real us to come to the surface and embody all that we were meant to be.

Mom did this for all twelve of her children. We are all very different, yet a common vein flows through us, and that is what our mom taught us. She taught us in her own way that, above all, you must follow your heart, even if it's scary to do so; that what you put out into the world comes back to you, but not necessarily in the way you think it would. She taught us to trust deeply, to have faith that all will work out no matter what, to give others the benefit of the doubt, to be honest, and to always take the high road.

I don't think as kids we knew how much these teachings would impact us and how our mom's lessons would translate into how we impacted others' lives. For that, Mom, I am forever grateful that you taught us to follow our hearts and let love be the cornerstone of all that we think, speak, and feel; to love ourselves, love our family, love our communities, love what we do to make a living, and love the world we are a part of even though it sometimes seems that love may not come back to us right away. When the COVID-19 pandemic began, I texted all of my siblings to say that I felt our childhood had completely prepared us for what was coming, and it has. When the human heart is at the center of all you put out into the world, everything falls into place, even in a pandemic, and things turn out better than you could have ever imagined. You just need to learn how to surrender into trusting your own heart, trusting your own knowing above anything else.

Mom, I am grateful that you taught me to follow my heart in my work because now we're impacting millions, all because you followed your heart and taught us to do the same.

My mom is the quintessential spiritual alchemist—Mary Murphy, the saint with twelve children.

Thank you, Mom! Love you!!
XOXO

THE PEOPLE INCLUDED
IN THIS BOOK

You will find numerous personal stories throughout *4 Spiritual Laws of Money!* Over the course of my career, I've been richly blessed with a colorful mosaic of clients and supportive team members. I'm continually amazed at the honesty, depth, and integrity of my clients and co-workers. Now it is my pleasure to share with you all of what we have learned together. To protect their privacy, the stories used throughout *The 4 Spiritual Laws of Money!* are composites of client histories and actual experiences represented by fictitious names. The case studies are based on the ways in which hundreds of people have navigated their financial and life planning, yet they do not apply to any one, specific, particular, identifiable individual.

I understand and value the power of personal stories and believe we learn most effectively through our own stories and those of others, particularly with lives that thrive. These selected vignettes capture the heart of this book and will be very helpful to you as you embark on your own journey in a whole new way, a new financial adventure, one that is created from the uniqueness of your heart and soul. I know you will be able to relate to many of these stories. By viewing wealth building through the lens of other people's experiences, your eyes will open to the infinite possibilities of a new reality for yourself, one filled with sustainable happiness, quality of life, prosperity, abundance, and inner peace.

TABLE OF CONTENTS

PREFACE

Why, on top of everything else going on in the world, am I being called to write another book? This question dogged me as I was completing a tumultuous divorce and part-time home-schooling my six-, eight-, ten-, and twelve-year-olds due to COVID regulations. I am the sole provider for my four young children as well as all the families that depend on me because I am their employer. *Yeah, let's just take on another thing,* I thought. All I could do was laugh.

For years, I've been guided to step into the unknown despite my highly educated brain saying to me, "Are you nuts? What are you thinking?" When it came to writing *The 4 Spiritual Laws of Money*, it was no different. I needed another thing to do like flying to the moon and back. Who's with me?

I've been a financial planner for nearly thirty years, running my own financial business since I was twenty-two years old. Over the years, I've realized that our financial system has forgotten about the human beings behind it all. We've built great financial products and education based on left-brain-logical analytics, but when it comes down to it, we've dehumanized finance. Considering all this, I began to ask myself, *How do we bring humanity back into finance?*

When I wrote my first book, *The Emotion Behind Money: Building Wealth From the Inside Out*, in 2008, people began asking me to speak in front of my peers as well as the general public. My industry colleagues met me with comments like "Wow, don't the younger people coming into the industry today have some interesting viewpoints?" Yet, when I would speak in front of thousands of people in the general public, I heard things like "I finally found someone who gets it!" Then I recognized, more than ever, that human emotions needed to be taken into account when coaching people about their money. This was a short-lived topic on the CNBC show *On the Money*, which I appeared on for about a year after the 2008-2009 recession. Once the world's economic numbers started performing again, CNBC canceled the show. I thought, *Wow, we have short-term memories of what created all this fiscal dysfunction in the first place: human emotions.*

Heck, when 70 percent of the economy is based on consumer spending, we'd better start considering all parts of the consumer, which includes their emotions as well as their logic. Prior to the 2008-2009 recession, people were buying homes they loved, but many of their home-buying decisions were not fiscally sound. When it came to their personal cash flow, many of them had no room to breathe. In many cases, every ounce of their income was accounted for. The bubble had burst collectively, and we created more financial heartache around the world.

Years later, *Harvard Business Review* published articles about behavioral finance. I believe this was a huge stepping stone for the industry. It was so important that it recognize that emotions are behind our money decisions and that the topic required more research and education. Meanwhile, I kept going even further down this rabbit hole. I started to drill down into why people make the same poor monetary decisions despite knowing that they need to make different decisions. I wanted to get to the bottom of it. I started to notice that emotionally, people not only acted out financially, but they also did this in other areas of their lives—in their relationships, their health, and their careers. People show up and respond to the world around them with the same emotional response system. Humans have two operating systems: the conscious mind and the subconscious mind. Research shows us that more than 97 percent of the time, we respond from the subconscious mind. So, what does this mean?

All humans experience some type of rejection or trauma before age seven. This then becomes the basis for every response we have to the world around us. It's coming from that little girl or little boy who didn't get their emotional needs met and now, they are reacting to the world from this emotional state only to keep repeating experiences in life, financially or otherwise. They are *still* trying to get their needs met. Understanding this dynamic helped me grasp why people stay locked up in debt cycles. I realized that people are trying to feel like they are "enough" or are trying to fill another emotional need through their spending. This realization helped me help my client base to achieve huge financial breakthroughs.

I use a whole brain approach—taking into account the left logical brain and the right emotional brain—when I work with clients. The financial breakthroughs they've achieved due to this approach inspired me to share it with the world. I thought, *Everyone deserves to create a life they love!* So, I wrote my second book, *Awaken Your Wealth: Creating a PACT to Optimize Your Money and Your Life*, which was published in 2019.

I've always said that we work things out or we act them out with our money, our relationships, and our health. When the pandemic hit in 2020, my online platform began to emerge in a whole new realm. I'm the money professional, and I had built a team of strategic partnerships to assist clients with other areas of their lives besides the financial area. I networked with what the industry would call "normal financial planner referral sources," like accountants, attorneys, and mortgage brokers; yet I also networked with a few that were a bit out of the box. They are professionals who help clients with areas including, but not limited to, health, relationships, career, and even the soul/spirit.

I saw that if clients didn't address these life areas, they would eventually manifest a life crisis that would force a shift.

I witnessed health crises, family crises, and career layoffs that devastated families. I asked myself, *Why can't we catch the headwinds of these crises and shift their lives BEFORE the crisis occurs?* That's what I started to do with clients, and it worked better than I could have imagined. With the aid of other experts, I helped clients figure out how to escape careers that were creating disease in their bodies and how to tackle other problem areas. I didn't expect the positive financial outcomes that resulted after they made their shifts.

Clients' financials improved more than they could have ever imagined. Their relationships were filled with more love, and they were in careers that fed their heart, soul, and wallet. They were lifted out of their suffering cycles. They returned to a place of inner empowerment. They were building their financial muscles from a whole different fuel source, one that was not fed from their unmet childhood needs but from a much more profound place, a place that was deep in their soul and they knew it.

As the pandemic continued to cause tremendous transformation around the world, people needed help. They were not only facing health crises, but also crises in their work lives, family lives, and, eventually as we all know, financially when the market hit its recession in 2020. Lives, workforces, communities, families, governments, and societies were imploding fast and were challenged like they've never been challenged before. So, I started to bring these other professionals at large to my social media channels to teach on a small scale to the masses.

Then, I heard the next part of my own personal calling: book number three.

We come into this world with an evolutionary path for our personal soul growth, that longing and urge that so many of us, financially sound or not, have inside that something is missing; something we just can't put our finger on. I'm here to tell you, it's your soul! We've left our hearts and souls on the sidelines for so many years, and the generations before us did the same. We turned over our personal power to things outside of ourselves, when the real gift is right inside each and every one of us! We've had the golden egg the whole time, but we've spent so much time distracting ourselves from it with debt, bad relationships, family drama, working too many hours at the cost of our families and communities, and the list goes on and on.

This is what led to my soul work and my calling to write *The 4 Spiritual Laws of Money*. I have an internal knowing that I came to this earth to create a major shift in how we handle money in our world today. We've allowed our debt structures to trap us in our lives working for a paycheck today to pay for yesterday and never really getting to the tomorrow we've always dreamed of despite all of the hard work. We've allowed our jobs to be the center of our lives at the cost of our families. We've lived so many years on autopilot. We've ignored the warning signs of poor health choices, eating food that is not as nourishing as it could be and sluggishly moving these vessels that keep us alive. The true gift of COVID-19 is that it put the brakes on the treadmill of life. It stopped it dead in its tracks and left us with the opportunity to create a whole new reality for ourselves and our loved ones.

You have the opportunity to create a reality that feeds you on every level of your being, fiscally, emotionally, spiritually, physically, and mentally. It's a level of wholeness that you have been searching for. Now, you know what foundation all these choices need to come from to give you sustainable fuel for happiness, joy, and peace. That fuel is you! Not someone or something outside of yourself, but you! It's that big, beautiful heart of yours to lead the charge into your new life, your new reality, one that you've always dreamed of having, creating happiness all along the way.

To get there, you have to open up to a new way of being and plugging into the world with your heart and soul. If you choose the path you've already taken, you will only get more of what you already have created. I'd love for you to understand what actually makes the world tick at its core and the foundational principles that can create quantum leaps for you in your life; and most importantly, how you most efficiently plug into them. *The 4 Spiritual Laws of Money* can get you there. It offers you a foundational basis that can give you such profound results that you'll wonder why it took you so long to get here. Know that your timing is *perfect*! You are *perfect*!

You deserve to go out and grab 100 percent of all that your heart desires.

INTRODUCTION

A LOT OF people talk about money in the following way: "If I only had the money to meet my bills, I would be happy." What happens though when you have enough money to meet your day-to-day expenses and are living comfortably yet you're still not happy? In today's world, where we regularly see billionaire power couples going through bitter divorces, it is obvious that monetary wealth alone is not enough to bring joy. This is because financial wealth alone does not make us happy. You can thrive financially and still have problems; those problems just come with a higher price tag. This is especially the case if you are not tuned in to your physical, emotional, intellectual, and spiritual being.

So, how do we get to feel happy and secure? Money helps us meet our basic needs, such as food, clothing, and shelter. But once we meet those needs, what does any amount of money do for us? It allows us to have choices. When you are working in a job you hate and barely scraping by, you, like most people, really don't want to risk trying something new or you are unwilling to start in an unknown situation if it means giving up a place of known security. Or, when you get laid off and don't have any money saved, you might jump into the first available job. That job may not be the best choice, but you accept it simply to meet your financial needs. This fear of not having financial security often comes full circle and may create a similar situation in your future. This is a case of the law of manifestation. You manifested what you were focused upon and directed your attention on getting a job to meet your basic needs. We will come back to this example in a little bit.

There are many factors in how money works for us besides the physical accumulation of wealth. They include the emotions of wealth, the intellectual thoughts of how we think about wealth, what "certain truths" our past patterns have taught us about wealth, and finally, our spiritual outlook on wealth. Wait, what? You can be spiritual *and* have financial wealth? Of course, you can! In fact, the sure way to gain both spiritual and material wealth is to follow your happiness and the path of unconditional love.

Today, as we are coming out of a global pandemic, we have had to spend a significant amount of time alone with our thoughts. People are coming into this new non-isolation world with a refreshed understanding about what makes them happy. So, they are starting to lead with their hearts and are waking up to the concept of the existence of unlimited potential in the world, including unlimited potential for wealth. This mindset shift is occurring because they are tuning further

into the knowing of their own awareness and are more willing to do something different.

We are all Spirit (God, Source, Creator, or whatever nomenclature you wish to use here), and we are all creators. Let's pause here and look at this again. *You are the creator of your life!* The first part of the creation process is envisioning what you desire or forming a picture of where you want to go.

Back to the previous job example. You could have quit that job at any time. It wasn't aligned with your happiness or bliss at all. This is what I call a pivot point or a crisis point. These points indicate that you are not following your heart or are not aligned with your higher self. At these crossroads, you have the chance to change your path. If you ignore these points, things will keep escalating, including your stress, anxiety, dissatisfaction, and depression. Finally, things come to a head, like in our example, in which you eventually get laid off. But once you have conquered your finances and accumulated enough money to cover your expenses and live comfortably, you give yourself the ability to have choice of where to go next to follow your bliss and your soul's purpose.

But if you had some wealth saved or you had less debt, you could have taken extra time to find a job more aligned with your higher self. Instead of marching on the endless treadmill of debt and living from paycheck to paycheck, you could break free of the cycle of struggling and onto the path your soul yearns for. The elimination of debt relieves you of a burden and gives you the power to choose the freedom of your soul. It allows you to leave a position with less risk because your expenses are lower. It allows you to follow your dreams with less perceived financial risk, therefore leaving you feeling safer. The next step in your journey enhances what you have already.

If this sounds familiar, it might be. Several years ago, I introduced readers to the PACT process. Don't worry if you didn't read *Awaken Your Wealth* as *The 4 Spiritual Laws of Money* doesn't require any knowledge of PACT. If you did read it, these laws also don't contradict this process. They dive deeper into the spirituality of money. PACT and the Spiritual Laws are like a muscle, where you take the steps one at time to build your real wealth. You envision what you want to manifest from your heart's desire and engage your heart to accept the reality of what you've created thus far. You free yourself energetically and then align your intention with your authenticity to redirect your energy to act upon your tailored vision. We need to realize that we are perfect exactly the way we are and we are right where we're supposed to be for our souls to evolve to the next level. Evolving is what we came here to do. We are in the perfect place and at the perfect time of our lives. We just need to take small steps, building that muscle a little at time. Celebrate each of the little wins and make adjustments that help you stay on your path, align with your soul, and raise you each time in sync with your higher self.

I have another example. A client of mine, Sandy, lived in one of the most fascinating historical places in Chicago. She loved the historical and architectural features of her building. She followed her bliss and interests to begin rehabbing architecturally unique and historical properties, and this truly sang to her. Once she rehabbed them, she rented them out. By following her happiness, she built a substantial property portfolio and built her own personal pension-like income plan for her retirement. Building this portfolio didn't seem like a struggle because she loved what she was doing. She created the pathway to her wealth, one that originated in her soul.

If you have read my other books, *Awaken Your Wealth* (2019) and/or its predecessor, *The Emotions Behind Money* (2008), and are curious about what's in this newest book, here you will find a deeper dive into building your real wealth and increasing your money along the way. You will learn to access your deep desire and purpose to get to your real wealth and how to make it work for you. You'll learn how to align it with your spiritual purpose. We will also look at the subject of real wealth from the viewpoint of someone who is more established in their life and spiritual viewpoint. I will show you what you can keep doing to reach your goals and feed your heart and soul whilst building your financial muscles each and every day.

Before we get to the meat of the book, I want to introduce you to the story of Natusha. Natusha embodies their name as a creative, original, visionary, people-oriented, and free-thinking individual. In Vedic astrology, Natusha is a person who listens to their heart more than their head. As you read this book, come back and think of these characteristics and how you can embody your own Natusha to help implement the 4 Spiritual Laws of Money. I want to leave you with this thought: You can create your life to be anything you want it to be. The possibilities are endless. The effort of this creation is significantly less if you align your desires to your life's purpose and bliss and appreciate the journey, not just the result. Lead with your heart, let go of the outcome once you have set the desire, align your actions with what you want to create, and then do your best to go out and get the life of your dreams. Let's begin!

*"There are only two days in the year
that nothing can be done.
One is called yesterday and the other
is called tomorrow.
So today is the right day to love,
believe, do and mostly live."*

—THE DALAI LAMA

*"There are only two days in the year
that nothing can be done.
One is called yesterday and the other
is called tomorrow.
So today is the right day to love,
believe, do and mostly live."*

—THE DALAI LAMA

CHAPTER 1

*"Imagination is everything.
It is the preview of life's
coming attractions."*

—ALBERT EINSTEIN

IN 2019, I introduced the PACT process, a system to help people bring money matters into the open and enable everyone to make a financial transformation. This process provides us with a format to revamp our relationship with money. It helps us understand that real wealth is not only about money. We achieve real wealth not only by having what we want and need but by feeling rich in every aspect of our lives—financially, emotionally, mentally, physically, and spiritually. PACT combines traditional financial strategies with introspection and creative innovation to reframe your individual relationship with money.

With the 4 Spiritual Laws of Money approach, the power of your heart and mind are combined to make money work for you to energize and create your desired life. As your life shifts to align with your heart, this has a quantum effect on your finances. As a result, your financial situation shifts and this opens up cash flow to allow you to pursue more of your passions. In essence, it creates the effect of a quantum leap in your life.

The 4 Spiritual Laws of Money are:

♡ Manifestation begins with desire.
♡ The heart is stronger than the brain.
♡ Intention redirects energy.
♡ The universe responds to action.

These laws are not a one and done tool. You can rely on them at any time in your financial lifecycle. Think of them as if you are peeling an onion. Each time you cycle through these laws and apply them to your life, you peel off a layer of your outer shell, getting deeper and deeper to your core and identifying what's *really* your truth. Every time you go through a cycle, you expand your consciousness and awareness and grow more into your authentic being on *all* fronts—physically, mentally, emotionally, and spiritually, not just financially. These 4 Spiritual Laws of Money can be individualized for your current situation, which might be a change in direction from previously using PACT. These four laws will also be valid ten years from now when you are at a different place in your life, both financially and spiritually. Even though your individual goals and situations change throughout your life, you can still look at your finances through the same spiritual lens. They are universal laws that stand the test of time.

Past and current spiritual leaders, hermits, and wise women/men have all taken walks in the wilderness or gone on a journey. Shamans and Native American spiritual leaders have embarked on many vision quests to find answers to raise themselves up. Think of the 4 Spiritual Laws of Money as your journey to find "real wealth."

The first stop is the first Spiritual Law: **Manifestation begins with desire.** This where you start picturing where you want to be, both financially and personally, living your heart's desire. Often, figuring out what you really desire is the most difficult step to take. Most of us know where we are now. We all know where we have been. But knowing where we want to go is sometimes harder to see. Let me help you with that.

Let's start with Lisa. Lisa is an accomplished woman, recognized and respected by her peers and her organization. She is strong, authentic, and has made a lot of headway in fighting her perceived limitations. Although she hasn't made it to the executive suite, something is giving her pause and she is not sure exactly why nor what to do about it, but she knows something needs to shift. But inside her subconscious, she is still apologizing for being herself and doesn't feel she can give up any more parts of "her" to hit the next level in her career. She appears to have herself together, but something is missing. She doesn't know what that something is because she can't yet see it. She just has this deep knowing or a yearning for something deeper, different, or more from her life.

You, like Lisa, need to get a vision of what you desire. Visualization is the ability to form mental pictures of abstract intentions and understandings. Using visualization, you see the picture of what you want to create in your life. You tune into a new, changed frequency in your brain. Research has shown that brain frequency is the starting point for manifesting your reality.

Look at what you really desire. Don't think in terms of what can and cannot be done. Do not let your ego limit you. You are never too late, too young, too entrenched, or too anything to stop from picturing a change in your future and going after your dreams. Tap into that beautiful heart of yours as it will give you all the answers you need.

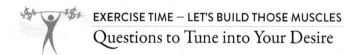

EXERCISE TIME – LET'S BUILD THOSE MUSCLES
Questions to Tune into Your Desire

So, how do you narrow down where to start? You are going to need a little time. For now, look within yourself and think about the direction you want to go to begin building your life filled with real wealth. Start by answering the brainstorming questions in this exercise time.

If we were sitting here three to five years from now, in your ideal world, what would that look like?

Every time I ask this question, people respond, "Do you mean financially?" I tell them that it doesn't matter. It could be financially, personally, professionally, familywise, or whatever comes to mind. Through the years, I have found it interesting that not one person has *ever* answered this by telling me where they want to be financially—at least, not as their first response. Why? Because, in most cases, our money isn't what drives us to deep, sustainable happiness. You never hear someone on their death bed say, "I wish I would have sacrificed and worked more to make more money." On their death bed, a person talks about the fact that they wish they would have worked less, treasured their loved ones more, or had more experiences. We long for more of that human connection, the experiences of life, and the ones not driven by material wealth, but rather time spent.

So, tap into that amazing heart of yours. You and I are sitting here three to five years from now. What does your heart desire?

- Who would you like to be spending it with, if anyone?
- What would you like to do be doing?
- Traveling?

- Any hobbies you'd like to take up that you've been putting on the back burner?
- Do you love your home?
- Would you like to live somewhere other than where you are now?
- What kind of job would you like to have?
- When do you want to retire?
- Where would you like to retire?

Stay in the dreaming piece of this process. Often, we can get stuck if we edit ourselves along the way when tapping into our hearts. Our minds will interrupt our process and not allow us to dream by negotiating with ourselves and telling us all the reasons why we can't do what our heart desires us to do, regardless of how crazy or unrealistic it may seem. Think of it as a brainstorming session where you are just vocalizing ideas. You will go back later and evaluate the ones you want to act upon. Remember, this process is about allowing yourself to take quantum leaps so you can avoid crises situations and embrace your soul's push for you to align with your heart.

- Would you like to financially support your kids, or other kids in your life, to get a higher education?
- Are you playing more financial defense versus offense? Would you like to shift that?
- What do you think of the debt you have, if any?
- Do you consider your debt to be good debt or bad debt? (Keep in mind, however, that all debt creates

a lack of freedom in the present moment to make choices.)

- ♥ Are you tired of being in debt?
- ♥ Would you like to have a plan to eliminate the debt?
- ♥ Do you want a different financial relationship? If so, what does that look like?

Often, we have a financial relationship that is based on the ghosts of our past. It's usually not a past that you even created. It's been handed down by the generations in the past along your lineage. These behaviors get passed down from one generation to the next in the form of limiting beliefs. These limiting beliefs get stored in our subconscious, and these patterns repeat over and over across decades.

- ♥ What new things for prosperity and growth do you have coming your way? And do you really resonate with these opportunities?
- ♥ Do the financial products you have or are looking to purchase support your personal financial intentions that you have *today*, not yesterday, but *today*?
- ♥ Do you make financial decisions based on fear? If so, how would you like to change that?
- ♥ What primary emotion/set of emotions do you feel at the exact moment you're about to buy your product or service? What specific words/phrases are you using as self-speak in your head? What story are you telling yourself?

- What do you secretly wish was true about your life situation, either as it relates to a product/service you're about to buy *or* in your life in general?
- What brands do you love (across any industry)? Why?
- What do you Google (list everything related to your business and your other interests)?
- If you had unstructured time, what would you be doing?
- What is your fantasy vacation? Why haven't you taken it? Would you like to change that?
- What things are you drawn to watch on YouTube that lift you into expansion and possibility?
- Who in your life reinforces or supports more of what you want to create in your life?
- Is there a part of your life where you'd like to come from more of a place of empowerment?
- Are you looking for a new relationship?
- If you are already in one, how do you feel when you are together? Is it your ideal partnership?
- Does your job excite you? If not, what would you like to change?
- Is the way you're living costing you your happiness?
- Do you find your happiness coming from what I call "external referral," meaning something outside of yourself that you need to do or someone you need to be with?
- Have you bulldozed your way into believing this is a good strategy, but you are still not where you want to be? If so, how do you see things differently today, and

would you like to shift to that way of plugging into the world instead of the way you've always done it?

♥ Do you feel you are on the verge of crossing into a highly desired space in your life? Why or why not?

♥ Do you feel like you're at a tipping point or that a bubble is about to burst?

♥ Are you distracting yourself from living your desired life?

♥ How do you distract yourself? Do you use food, alcohol, cigarettes, people-pleasing, or over giving? Are you addicted to work, exercise, or any other vice? What keeps you distracted from your heart and feeling those feelings?

♥ Are you seeking something different? What is it?

♥ Are you ready to soar to your highest potential in this lifetime?

♥ Can you find the courage to be your true authentic self all the time?

♥ Do you feel you have no life outside work? If yes, is that the way you want it to be? If no, then what does your ideal work world look like?

♥ Do you wake up and realize the life you have isn't the dream? What would you like to shift to make your dreams your reality?

♥ What else can you do to fully love yourself, to really come from a place of extreme self-love and self-care?

♥ What part of your life feels like being in your own personal prison? Your job? Your relationship? Marriage? Family life? Would you like to bust the chains that bind you? If so, what is the opposite of that prison you've created?

♥ What makes you find joy or that amazing giggle? What leaves you feeling content?

♥ When did you last feel that time flew by like it was nothing? What were you doing?

♥ When was the last time you felt excited or passionate about what you were doing? What was it?

♥ Do a gut check on your answers. Do they feel and sound right to you? A few nerves or excitement about where you are going is fine, but if something makes you sick, anxious, feels wrong, or even just gives you pause, it is probably not where you want to go.

Keep at it until you feel good about your answers, even a little excited, in both your head and your heart. Take these answers, read over them, meditate, and feel the feelings that you will have once all your desires come into manifest form. It only takes three minutes per day to put your hand on your heart and breathe in slowly through your nose, out through your mouth. Then feel, in your heart, the feelings as if all has already come into being. Easy-peasy! This kind of feeling meditation, tapping into and activating your heart within, will help validate and solidify in the mind that this is what you truly want, and from there, this enables you to create your vision.

Using your answers, you now need to build a picture of what you desire. But how do you do that? If you can see in your mind what you desire, great! Some of our minds can be very distracting. I know that to be true for myself. If you need a little more help to see the picture, consider several other ways to refine your view.

If words are your first response, journal what you want and use the words to craft the picture. Sometimes, putting pen to paper helps you see the message in a physical form.

♡ If you are a more visual person, gather images from your meditation as ideas of the direction you want to go. If your meditation doesn't usually take a visual route, then create a vision board with pictures cut out and arranged meaningfully on a poster board. You can also do a virtual vision board using Pinterest or the Canva website. You can choose from so many options, and there is never a right or wrong way to approach this. Just pick the option that resonates the most and allow it to feel easy and simple.

♡ I will never forget my first time creating a vision board. A few other women business owners and I hired a group business coach, Karyn Pettigrew, to take us to the next level in our businesses as well as our personal lives. During one of our first gatherings, Karyn told us all to grab some magazines and art materials to create a vision board. Keep in mind, at the time I was a full-fledged left-brained financial planner. I was very much in my go-getter masculine energy where it was all about the numbers, not about art! I didn't identify at all with the creative side of my being. I was missing the most magical part of who we are as human beings: the mystery part, the part that on many levels, through all my formal education and training, I had shut down. I relied more on my brain and my thoughts to solve my next steps in life. Wow, was I mistaken! Sound familiar?

I was all about pushing up to the next level in creating my business and wanting to be better than most of my colleagues. I was a mover and shaker, and it completely dumbfounded me how cutting pictures out of a magazine would take me higher in both my career and personal growth. Being a people-pleaser at the time, I sat politely looking through the magazines while hiding my feelings of complete annoyance. I couldn't believe we had hired this chick. To this day, Karyn and I laugh about it; the silly things we think when we are stuck in our own way of plugging into the world! If I only knew then how I was plugging into the world with the wrong fuel source to activate my desires. I was only using my mind, and I was leaving my heart out of the equation. I had no idea I was doing this.

That day, Karyn proceeded to say, "Okay, we only have about fifteen more minutes, so you may want to start cutting the items out of the magazines and gluing them down on your vision board." Little did I know that this would be a major turning point for me. This process back-doored my linear, left, highly educated and trained logical brain and showed me what my subconscious mind and heart were starving for. I was so busy pushing my way through life that I was completely

missing the boat. I have so much gratitude for the grace Karyn bestowed on me during this session. That day, I learned a concept I mentioned in the preface—that we have two operating systems as human beings: our conscious mind and our subconscious mind. Most of the time, our subconscious is running the show. The subconscious is usually not occupied with what we truly desire. It operates from our childhood rejection or trauma and causes us to repeat our personal suffering using our limiting belief patterns.

So, a vision boarding experience opens the door to what is deeply true for us in our hearts and not our suffering patterns. It gets us out of our heads. Keep in mind that our brains don't give up that easily. What do I mean? I became the best damn competitive vision board maker around! I don't do anything small. I had probably twenty of them, and then Spirit woke me! Another coach of mine—an energy healer, if you will, Anne Emerson—pointed out to me that I had turned my vision boarding into a left-brain linear process. I kept making the boards to manifest my desires but didn't realize that things change constantly as we evolve. So, the vision was true for me when I made the boards, but it may have only been a stepping-stone to getting to the next place in my evolution.

I realized I had turned my vision boarding into a suffering cycle again, triggering my "not enough" button. My brain had hijacked the process. I was missing one big, vital component. I didn't realize it until Anne said to me, "Your homework from Spirit is to burn your vision boards." I immediately responded,

"Are you nuts?" I had found a gateway to my spirituality that worked for me, and I had so much resistance to her telling me I had to burn them. Look "how much work" I had done. But I've learned that once resistance shows up, you are right up against your limiting belief; you're fighting that unwanted programming and prohibiting baggage. This signals that you're about to experience a major shift in your life. The more resistance you feel, the bigger the transformation will be. It was time to push through that resistance. I knew it on every level. The baggage that you are carrying is holding you back from manifesting your desires because you are in your limited-belief suffering patterns. You can either stay in your pattern and be stubborn and stuck or find the courage to release how or why doing something as simple as burning your vision boards can quantum leap you to the next place. I've found that, often, spiritual solutions are low-cost, easy, and simple yet are met with extreme resistance from our inside.

My husband at the time thought I was nuts. My eldest child was about one and a half years old, and I was pregnant with baby number two when I took my vision boards out on the balcony, tore them up, and burned one piece at a time. I sobbed gut-wrenching tears pulled from the depths of my being. I could see why someone would think this was an over-the-top reaction, but I had learned something dramatic: To manifest your desires, you must detach from the outcomes you're trying to manifest. It's not for you to figure out how the manifestation comes into form. Spirit, the Universe, God—whatever higher power resonates with you—has your back all the time. Once you trust that and release the attachment you have to the outcome (like I did with the magazine pictures on my vision boards), all will come into manifest form and reality. Your job is to feel the feelings deep within your heart as if your life has already had your desires met.

 EXERCISE TIME — LET'S BUILD THOSE MUSCLES
Meditation to Add to Your Manifestation Picture

If you need more help putting a clear picture in your mind of your new life direction, use the visualization exercise here to help you craft your vision.

Guided visualization exercise: Have someone read this to you slowly, or feel free to record the words to replay to yourself so you can relax while doing this visualization.

Begin by closing your eyes and picturing the story as it unfolds. Calm your mind and body. Concentrate on your breath. Take several deep breaths in and out, in and out. Do this ten times. Sometimes, it helps to breathe in to the count of five, pause for two beats, and then breathe out to the count of eight. This slows down your nervous system and drops you more into your heart, your feeling space. Picture someone you admire. Visualize what they are doing. Take note of their appearance, their smile, and how much fun they are having. Observe where they are, what they are doing, and who is around them. Continue to breathe in and out and watch the scene play out.

Now, put yourself in the scene. Picture your smile. What are you doing? Feel free to change the vision to something that brings you more joy. Note the day's weather. What do you smell? Who is with you? What do you hear? What feelings are your heart aligning with? Spend several minutes watching the scene, letting your heart guide the vision toward where you want to go. Let your heart feel your happiness and experience your joy. Let yourself drift in the vision. Let imagination create the picture of where your heart wants to go. If your brain or ego tries to interrupt with criticisms or questions, let them slide away. Continue to observe. Sit inside yourself, and watch your thoughts, dreams, and desires play out. After a time, when you feel at peace, concentrate on your breath again. Feel your body where you are, and breathe in and out five more times. When you are ready, open your eyes and capture what you saw in your journal, on paper, or through recording it while it is still fresh in your mind. Use this information to craft your vision and launch the new version of you.

Now, let's go back to Lisa, the accomplished upper midlevel professional we encountered a few pages ago who has her life together but is not living as her authentic self. She has created wealth, through income affluence and assets, but not *real wealth*. She's yearning for something more from life, and up to this point, she has not been able to put her finger on what that "more" is. She answers the questions and then realizes that teaching is where her passion lies. She feels she has a way of conveying hard subjects in simple terms. She enjoys passing knowledge onto others and the intellectual stimulation of people discussing new concepts. In her mind, she has a strong picture of herself teaching at a small university. Is there anything else she needs to do as part of the **manifestation begins with desire** law?

As a part of that picture, you and Lisa need to consider what your personal intentions are to create real wealth. What is going to make you happy and feel satisfied? Think about the quality of your life instead of the drive to make more income or the quantity of your assets. Look at not just your financial picture but all aspects of your life, such as family and other relationships, your work and your health. How do you want your world to look? Do you want to be more in service of others? Keep in mind, this doesn't mean you go broke and live just above poverty level. This is such a myth! We don't have to forgo financial success to follow what our heart is longing to do; we can have both. We just need to set the intention, feel the feelings as if our intention is a reality, and then allow it to manifest in our lives. Look for clues to things that make you giggle or put a happy smirk on your face. Remember, don't evaluate or judge what pops in, just let it flow out of you and stay in your mystery! I get that you don't know "how" it will come into being, but for now, please, do yourself a favor and stay in the mystery. You're safe. It's okay, and you got this! Ask yourself this: *How do I participate in the oneness of the world in my own way with my own gifts?* The sky is the limit!

So, now, for that dream life, the one where you are living on your own terms, how do you want to use your gifts? Yes, everyone has gifts! It's not enough to manifest what you desire (for example, how much money you have and the lifestyle and abundance you want), it needs to bring *you* happiness, joy, and laughter along the way. You need to be able to enjoy the journey.

There's little point in having all the money you desire if you still experience a deep longing and emptiness. In my career, I've met enough multimillionaires who are rich but empty—so unhappy and deeply unfulfilled. You need to take a good long look inside your heart and that means going within. Meditate or walk outside and connect with nature; listen to more than just your brain with its concrete black and white lines. If it's really challenging to hear your heart and what it truly desires, just put your hand on your heart and ask it what it wants. It will offer you all the answers.

I realized that I had ignored my own heart's desires because I was people-pleasing regularly. I was showing up for everyone else in the world except myself. It may take a while, a few days, weeks, or maybe even a month of daily practice of putting your hand over your heart and asking it what it desires. Be patient. Your heart is not used to being heard. You've rolled over it for years with your monkey mind. Give it time to open, and I assure you, it will. Think of it as building a muscle. Every day you do this exercise, it gets stronger. Your heart, after all, is a muscle, and everyone knows you build muscles with

exercise. At this stage, remove any kind of ego-driven thinking plan and use all the colors inside the toolbox of your heart. Once you do, it just keeps flowing and feels amazing!

"Watch your thoughts, they become your words;
watch your words, they become your actions;
watch your actions, they become your habits;
watch your habits, they become your character;
watch your character, it becomes your destiny."

—LAO TZU, ANCIENT CHINESE PHILOSOPHER

As I stated in the introduction, you are a Creator and can create whatever you desire. It is not just a matter of picturing it. Remember the last spiritual money law: **The universe responds to action.** However, the first law is **manifestation begins with desire.** By directing your thoughts, words, and feelings, you invoke the Law of Attraction where your thoughts attract similar thoughts and opportunities. So, if you think positive thoughts, you attract positive outcomes. If you focus on negative thoughts and what can't be done, you create a self-fulfilling prophecy of negativity. Think of the Law of Attraction like putting an order in with Source (God, Spirit, Goddess, Creator, or whatever nomenclature you wish to use here) and allowing Source to look around and find the best match for your manifestation. The same is true for your words and feelings. Like attracts like, so let's ensure that all of our words, thoughts, and feelings are high vibrational. For this to have the most optimal outcome, you have to know authentically what you want and picture it in your mind. Most importantly, you must feel it in your heart as if it's already here.

Once you have the picture in your mind, focus on what you want to *create* instead of the problems of getting there or the ones you already have. The Law of Attraction says you draw to you what you focus your energy and vibration on. As previously stated, you decide where you want to go, and Source decides the method to get you there. Trust comes into play here. Detach from what you have always known as the one way to do or achieve a complex task or goal. Release some of what you have been taught. Let go of the outcome, detach from how all will manifest, and believe and trust that all will align and show up. Focus on what you can control, and trust that the opportunities will come. Then, step into action.

Do you know the number-one limiting belief people have about money? That there is not enough—that there has to be those who have and those who have not. Why is there not enough? Who told us this story? It is just that—a fictional story, one that we've chosen to believe on some level? Many people have made more money than anyone thought possible in this generation. Look at Oprah Winfrey, Jeff Bezos, or Bill Gates. They are just the tip of the iceberg! You need to work on the belief that financial abundance existence for *everyone*, not just a select few.

You are enough.

You are worthy.

You are loved.

You are Source.

You are the creator of your life.

And *you* deserve financial abundance too.

But how do you know? How do you figure it out? Look within your heart and gut, not just within your brain. Create space in your life to tune into yourself by walking outside, meditating, going for a run, or doing whatever else puts you in that meditative state. You know what does it for me sometimes? Watching a fire, whether it's a candle, my fireplace, or an outside campfire. I also create space from my monkey mind by doing a puzzle. Oh, the inspirations and messages I get from Spirit while I do puzzles are simply amazing! I find myself in the zone that allows me to tap into the meditative gap. I connect into the higher realms of my being and tune into higher guidance, and you can too! It's super easy! Give yourself some unstructured down time in your calendar to just "be" and visualize. This allows you to tune into your all-knowing, to get out of your head, and to follow what brings you happiness and joy. You can only get to this place of happiness by bringing your authentic self along for the ride of your life's journey.

Do you know that more neurons exist in your gut than your head? Your gut sends more messages to your body than your brain. So, why aren't we taught from an early age to trust our gut over our brains? We don't feel safe on some level, and when we don't feel safe, we look for something outside of ourselves to provide that safety; hence, we go to our minds and try to figure the problem out. The challenge of relying just on the mind, however, is that its rationale is shaped by our trauma or rejection before we were seven years old. Our different experiences are just part of our being human, hard-wired into our subconscious mind, which is running the thought engine 97 percent of the time. It forms the basis for how we react to the world.

Think of it like a jigsaw puzzle. Have you ever put a piece in a spot that you swore was the right one, then you got stuck because you couldn't finish putting all the pieces together to complete your masterpiece because that one piece was actually in the wrong spot? Your life is the same. If you are coming from a place where the subconscious mind, your reactive side, is running your life, you'll never put all the pieces together seamlessly. Even if you put together a lot of your life, it will be like the puzzle—a masterpiece unfinished. The key is to solve the mystery of what you are yearning and searching for, and you have to trust your gut. By trusting your gut, your inner knowing, and your intuition, you will get more of what you desire. You can watch the puzzle of your life come into the perfect picture, which will be deep joy and happiness. Do this in bite-size pieces to feel safe as you build that muscle of trusting your gut. This gives you the opportunity to reconnect with yourself and reconnect with Spirit as opposed to how everyone else wants you to show up in the world. Your all-knowing self is where all vibrations of your wants, desires, and needs reside.

How can you keep thinking positively? You could do affirmations such as "I am abundant" or "I am (whatever dream you have pictured)." As you say these, *feel* the feelings as if you're already abundant and as if all the other dreams you have pictured for yourself have come true. Affirmations bring your positive pictures to the forefront of your heart and mind. They vibrationally confirm your vison with purpose, keeping you on track to obtain your goals. They enable the Law of Attraction to do its work and draw more complementary opportunities toward you. Put these affirmations in your phone reminders or on your to-do list. You can even change your passwords according to your monetary goal to keep your picture at the forefront of your heart and mind.

Another positive practice is feeling and expressing gratitude in a journal or out loud for the things you have and the vision you are working toward. Scientists have now proven that our emotions can be measured as high vibration or low vibration. As you can imagine, gratitude, along with joy, happiness, and love, are all high vibration. When your positivity is in the forefront of your heart and mind, you will see coincidences that align with your goals. These really aren't coincidences but opportunities to manifest your dreams. They are signs of your progress!

You can also use a manifestation journal, which is a written record of what you want to occur. This journal-keeping fuels your intention. It helps to activate the Law of Attraction. Journaling daily can help switch your scarcity mindset to an abundance mindset.

Let's return to Lisa. To keep her positive feelings and thoughts going, she began keeping a gratitude journal for what she has. She also picked three affirmations to concentrate on:

- ♡ I am enough.
- ♡ I am wisdom.
- ♡ I am a teacher.

She has already generated a new opportunity of being a mentor to the new interns at work, and she has put this in her gratitude journal.

What did you decide to do to keep your positivity going? Have you ever considered cutting back on or no longer talking to and hanging out with people who don't support your new life vision? I refer to these types of people who don't support or align with my new vision as "the crabs in my bucket." This is because they try to pull me down. In contrast, have you proactively aligned with others who share your desired visions of your life direction now that you've created more cash flow? Aligning with others who support our vision and taking tactical steps in the direction of our heart's desires always creates more space for new opportunities and experiences. You are the company you keep! Sometimes, that's hard to see, but it's true.

Just like paying off a debt, when you no longer need to make that payment, where do you want that money or intention to flow? Clients tell me all the time, "Julie, we called you because everyone is telling us all the reasons we can't do 'X' and we knew you'd help us find a way to see the bigger picture and how to get there." And . . . we do!

Are you ready to learn about the next Spiritual Law? If so, it's time to move forward.

CHAPTER 2

"Being in your element is not only about aptitude, it's about passion: it is about loving what you do . . . tapping into your natural energy and your most authentic self."

—SIR KEN ROBINSON

WE MOVE FORWARD now upon our journey to the second Spiritual Law of Money: **The heart is stronger than the brain.** So far, our journey has helped us understand that manifestation begins with heart-centered desire. Now, we will take a deeper dive into where we are with our hearts and not our heads. Self-acceptance is the act or state of recognizing and affirming oneself. It is recognizing your own abilities without judgment, meaning that your ego and your brain do not get the final say in who you are. They are only part of that equation, and if I say so myself, it's the second half of the equation! "Start with your heart and then add your smarts," as my mentor Deirdre Morgan says.

Self-acceptance is about acknowledging who and where you are and that you are the creator of exactly where your life is at this point. Breathe that in. Yes, it's deep! And, I know it's hard to hear, so let me say it again—*you are the creator of your life*. You have created, or your ego may prefer the word co-created (mine did), every single ounce of reality that stands in front of you. Take another deep breath to absorb the realization that you are the creator of your life, and allow that to sink in a little deeper within your body. You have created your life—*all* of it! That is a tough pill to swallow, I know, but bear with me.

Authenticity is being true to one's own heart, personality, spirit, or character. Authenticity is knowing who you are in your heart and having the courage to allow this version of yourself to rise to the surface and be in tune with what makes your soul happy. This enables you to understand how you want to journey in your own life and find the courage to do it. Living authentically will fuel your success. None of us knows how our success will all show up. This uncertainty is the point where our minds and egos start messing with us. I have seen it time and time again. When you choose *you*, in all your truth and authenticity, everything rises up and increases—more money, more love, and way more happiness come into being.

It's almost as if when success arrives, you just want to pinch yourself because it makes you feel so giddy and alive on a level you've never experienced.

The first step is your acceptance of self. Accept all the good, the bad, and the ugly, every ounce of it! Take a deep breath. Just breathe into it. You got this! You just need to look at the now without any shame, blame, guilt, or judgment. Accept your current reality and observe all the stress, strain, and resistance that may arise. I understand that you may have financial statements you don't want to open because you don't want to acknowledge the reality of the current situation. I always say you either work things out or act them out through your money, health, or relationships. Perhaps your ugly is showing up in your relationships. If so, accept this dysfunction. Or your addiction to work causes you to keep pushing your way through the rat race of life only to take a toll on your health more and more as you age.

I know there is at least one decision you would love to go back and change. Reality is what it is! Breathe into that . . . allow any emotions that want to come up to do so. Say out loud to yourself, "I accept my reality. I accept my reality. I accept my reality." Keep affirming this until it provokes an emotion inside of you. By saying this out loud, your body opens up and releases any blocked emotions. Feel them. Feeling these emotions from your past, which have been buried deep within you, is how you accept your reality. Feel these feelings as this is the only way to get to the other side.

Once you have unearthed and felt the buried feelings, take another deep breath and say to yourself, "It's okay. I'm okay. I am safe." Please understand, we can only do something about the here and now, not yesterday. Choosing to not accept your reality only keeps you manifesting your past all over again, which then creates the same results and outcomes. You can't change the past. You can only look at this current moment because it's the only thing you've got. Anything else you tell yourself is just a story and *not* your truth. You are here in this place *now* and your situation is what it is. I realize that many emotions are tied up with how you got to this place. Keep allowing yourself to feel the feelings of your reality to create more space for the new.

The only way to the other side of your patterning is through it. No more dancing around and finding other unsuccessful strategies to attempt to dodge the patterns. You might be wondering what I mean by "through." It's about feeling the feelings that have gone for years buried and unfelt. By not releasing these feelings, they crystalize in our physical bodies. These crystallizations create physical disease after years of not processing the emotions. Let's hold a safe space for ourselves and hold the space to clear any of our judgments. We are going to love with all our hearts and accept ourselves and our situation as it stands in this moment. So often, we only do this for others, but why not do it for ourselves first and foremost? Well, now's the time. You matter, and the world is waiting for you to show up in the perfect form that you were made to be!

In the past, you might have responded with a knee-jerk or nervous reaction. Not this time! Take a deep breath, take one mental step back, and breathe into the emotions that arise and release them. As I mentioned, the only way to step into your new reality is through all those messy emotions you've not been able or willing to feel. Sometimes, we don't even recall the event or experience these emotions are tied to. And I've come to learn that it doesn't matter where they originated, I just want to let them go and release them with ease and grace. I wasn't always in this space though. It took time for me to release that left, logical, smart brain of mine that wanted to understand and figure it all out so I had all the answers. I'm just not interested in doing so any longer as it's another distraction to prevent me from living a life that I absolutely love. I just want to embody *exactly* what my soul came here to do in this lifetime.

When looking at your current situation, drop into the meditative higher-self space you experienced when you were picturing what you wanted to manifest within the first Spiritual Law. To do that, just drop into your heart center either through slowly breathing in and out, meditating, walking outside in nature, praying, dancing, or pursuing any other creative outlet that creates space. Remember, for me, puzzles put me in a meditative state. Just be open. There is no textbook or single way to do this. Your way is perfect. Just do whatever gets you out of your monkey mind.

Consider sitting quietly and centering your energy within yourself. Concentrate on your breath. Breathe slowly. Observe any emotions that come up, then let them rise from inside and feel them release and pass through as you focus on your breath and yourself in that moment. Once you drop into your heart-centered space, you are ready to take a closer look at your current situation.

In *Awaken Your Wealth*, I outlined how to look at your current financial situation by tracking your past, present, and future financial timeline. I also outlined how I recommend for you to approach your daily, weekly, monthly, and annual expenses to get a realistic view of your current financial flow.

 EXERCISE TIME – LET'S BUILD THOSE MUSCLES
Your Current Situation

Let's clarify your financial picture.

- ♡ Gather all your statements and financial information in one place.
- ♡ Record debt, cash flow coming in, cash flow going out, and your assets.
- ♡ Add up each column with totals along the bottom (see the following figure).

FINANCIAL TIMELINE

PAST	PRESENT	FUTURE
Debt	Cash Flow	Assets

Track the following:

- ♡ Daily expenses
- ♡ Weekly expenses
- ♡ Bills paid monthly
- ♡ Annual bills: Don't forget to include these as they can really throw cash flow for a loop when they are due (see the following figure).

DAILY EXPENSES	WEEKLY EXPENSES	ANNUAL BILLS

BILLS PAID MONTHLY

Housing	
Mortgage/Rental	$
HOA & Maintenance	$
Utilities	$
Property Taxes	$
Housing Total	$
Transportation	
Loan/Lease	$
Fuel	$
Service	$
Insurance	$
Transportation Total	$
Medical Expenses	
Medical	$
Dental	$
Mental	$
Medications	$
Medical Total	$
Totals	$

Accepting your current situation is a game-changer because without accepting where you are, you can never move forward into the life you want. When you refuse to open those statements and acknowledge the way you are regularly spending your money, creating debt, or creating lack of accumulation of money, you are resisting to recognize where you currently are.

You create your world, so if you resist being aware of your problems and feeling all the feelings behind your reality, that situation will persist. It's as they say, "If you do what you've always done, you'll get what you've always gotten." It'll come with different people, faces, names, and situations, but it's all the same patterning—until you interrupt the pattern. This also pertains to your personal, work, and family life. Since knowledge is power, when you reach that place of acceptance, you step into your full potential and live from a place of empowerment. It removes your resistance, which kept your blinders on, and helps you view the situation without the rose- or charcoal-colored lenses of emotion.

Facing your current reality can be the hardest part of this law. It's also the biggest breakthrough! Everything in life has its light and dark sides. Let's focus on the light side, the part that creates expansion in our lives. Often, it's a grieving process for many. It certainly was for me. It's okay that this process brings up the emotions that surround how you spend your money, live, or share your life with others or the place that you work that no longer feeds your soul. It's time for you to acknowledge

BILLS PAID MONTHLY

Housing	
Mortgage/Rental	$
HOA & Maintenance	$
Utilities	$
Property Taxes	$
Housing Total	$

Transportation	
Loan/Lease	$
Fuel	$
Service	$
Insurance	$
Transportation Total	$

and witness these emotions. This may be especially true for decisions that you've made and would likely change a second time around and the problems that resulted, which you had to scale or are currently scaling. After all, they have brought you to where you are today. And know that where you've been is absolutely perfect because it got you to where you are and provided the growth in your soul's vibration.

It's okay to acknowledge heartfelt emotions when thinking about how these decisions have affected you. Once you acknowledge them, however, let them go and release the attachment or addiction to them because ultimately those decisions and emotions are in the past. Yes, I said "addiction" to those emotions. What? We can be addicted to more than food, alcohol, drugs, cigarettes, etc. Yep, emotional addictions are a real deal.

You don't consciously choose to be addicted to your emotions, but your physical body is. Let's say you seem to always find yourself in a place of drama with others. Due to your subconscious response/reactive system, you respond to the world from your buried trauma or rejection before you were seven years old. Remember us talking about that earlier? That drama then creates tension, frustration, sadness, anger, fear, and so on. When these lower vibrating emotions permeate around your physical system, your body creates cortisol. Cortisol gives you a boost, or high, inside. You then become addicted to the cortisol pumping through your veins, therefore creating a deeper pattern over time. Yet, it all can be released. I know because I've done it. For you too, after you put these emotions in your rearview mirror, you can truly live in the present moment.

You are in the ***now***, the present moment, because that is all that ever is, and what is past can no longer be changed. So, let's operate from a place where we stop bringing our past into our lives in the present moment. Why? Because then the past becomes the basis of the future we are creating. Choose the new desires you have *now*, not yesterday's regrets and frustrations, as the foundation to create your tomorrow. Once you surrender to the fact that those situations and emotions are no longer going to define your future and are officially only in your past, this deeper acceptance will allow your energy to free up and expand. Wow, it feels incredible! We all only have so much energy. How do you want to allocate or spend it? This newfound freedom allows you to vibrate higher and attract more of what you desire because you are no longer spending that energy on regret or churning the "what if" cycle around on your past choices.

Our example, Lisa, does this exercise, and she realizes that her finances are in pretty good shape. But she's in a cycle that I call the hybrid model. She spends half her time in financial scarcity and the other half in financial abundance—a financial seesaw. Debt levels go up and down, cash flows are great sometimes and challenging in others. There is no steadiness in building her assets to lead Lisa to her goals. Sound familiar? Lisa makes a good income and has been paying down her debt.

However, when she looks at her work life, she knows that the next logical step is to be an executive because that is the pinnacle of the business world and it follows all she has been educated and trained to do. After all her hard work, she is not there, and in her heart, she is not sure she has what it takes to get there or at least not getting there by the same methods that created her current reality. This frustrates her beyond belief, like she chose the wrong career or the wrong company, and she feels she is not enough. She's spent so much time and energy plowing and pushing her way up to the next level, with good intent, and thought she was always doing the right thing only to find herself in a scarcity consciousness once again.

Lisa sits back, drops into her heart-centered space, and looks at the now. She has income affluence and has created some financial wealth, but not *real wealth*. She is a successful businesswoman. Yet, she is not in the job or career that truly makes her happy. She knows something is missing but just can't put her finger on it. She's being called to something with bigger purpose and passion.

Let me give you another way to look at this. Everything and everyone in this world is energetically connected. You, me, and your next-door neighbor are all connected, even if you don't like them, agree with them, or even though you've never met each other! Think of the whole world as an energy grid, where all the lines are connected to every other energy point (each individual person). Visualize this by thinking about when you have flown into a big city like Chicago or

Atlanta. Upon your approach to the airport, you look down at the city and see that all the streets are laid out and connected. You see the lights (energy) traveling down those streets to touch other places and people. You see how the city is linked in various ways. The world is much the same.

What if a breakdown occurs in one part of that city, such as a transmitter blowing or a big wreck happening on the highway, blocking all the traffic lanes? You notice the energy stops moving not just at the point of the problem but in all the surrounding areas. One single point in the grid affects all the other points because we are all connected. For example, when I got divorced, I was going to weekly sessions with someone whom I would call a mentor, my guru and my teacher, Panache Desai. I had been doing one-on-one sessions with him since December 2015, and it was now August 2018. I had gotten divorced that prior week, and the first thing Panache said to me during our weekly session was "Thank you!" I was so confused. I felt like I had been through absolute hell getting divorced, attacked by the legal system, and experiencing a massive emotional hangover. I asked him, "Why are you thanking me?" He said, "You have made it easier for every other woman who is still in a marriage similar to yours, one based on both parties not showing up as their true authentic selves, to take an authentic action. You've opened up the energy grid."

At the time, I really didn't understand what he was talking about, but over the next few months and still to this day, women come out of the woodwork to ask me how I found the courage to leave my marriage and how I did it. In hindsight, my experience and wisdom allowed their paths to be easier. The energy grid opened up; I now see exactly what Panache was talking about.

The grid of human connectedness is the same; one point can affect all the other points. You can't control your neighbors' behavior or energy flow, but you *can* control your own. Your main concern in the energy grid should be focused on yourself, operating from a place of extreme self-love and self-care. This particular wisdom may go against what we have been taught to take care of our neighbor and our brothers before ourselves. However, let's get back on a plane. The first thing that the flight attendant tells you, when everyone is seated, is about safety and the procedures if something goes wrong. In this speech, the flight attendant says that if oxygen becomes necessary, you must put your own mask on before assisting others with theirs. In other words, you need to take care of your needs to be in a position to help someone else.

The same can be said about the interpersonal energy grid. If your energy is low or diminishing, it is going to bring the energy of the others around you down. But if you raise your energy by taking care of your own needs, you raise your energy *and* the energy of the entire grid around you. Again, remember we can't control how anyone else's energy affects the grid, but because we are all connected, we can use our own energy to uplift ourselves, which in turn uplifts everyone else. I know, it sounds counterintuitive, but that is how it works.

Let's look at it from another vantage point. What if you choose not to stay in your own energy lane? Meaning, someone who is being judgmental and angry triggers you because they are coming from a different vantage point than what you believe to be true. There's lots of that going on in our world today, right? We can see it everywhere. When you join them in that energetic exchange, you shift to their lower vibration and you darken or lower the overall energy grid. Does that make sense? It can go both ways. Oftentimes, many of us don't realize how by not staying in our energetic lane, meaning being authentically ourselves in our heart, we choose to show up in the way that others are showing up. Therefore, we are not operating at our highest vibration.

If you're at a place of happiness and joy because you are showing up authentically in the world, this is how you most effectively create positive change. It's not about changing others, it's about changing yourself. It's all proven now by quantum physicists and biologists. We are absolutely truly amazing beings! We are all living in a quantum field of energetic intelligence that we've barely tapped into.

What else steals our energy? When we concentrate on everything we have done wrong and get mired in the emotions of our "bad" decisions, we waste our energy on a past we cannot change. You are a creator, so when you concentrate on bad

outcomes and things that are wrong, you are going to drag more of those bad outcomes toward you. You keep repeating your past, financially, in relationships, with different bosses, to name a few examples. You also expend a substantial amount of energy going to work to earn a paycheck. The flow of energy used in earning a paycheck is diverted away from you to your creditors when you have accumulated debt. Think of debt payments as a leaky container for your current cash inflows. Without debt, your paycheck energy flow stays with you in the present moment and can be used for your desires and plans today, not paying for all your choices of yesterday and your past. Where your cash flows, your energy goes and you choose. Choose to have debt and vacations, or create financial space to work less in the future to provide for yourself and your loved ones.

Why is having low energy a big deal? Well, without energy, nothing gets done. You don't go anywhere or do anything. Low energy leads to depression and isolating yourself from others. Financially, it also means you don't deal with your patterns, which could lead to more debt—a lead balloon holding you back, bosses you don't like, raises and bonuses you missed that you deserve, or divorce again and half of what you built going out the door when the ex does, and the circle repeating itself.

Using your energy for your life and tying it back to accepting your current situation is crucial, but how else can you improve the energy flow besides reducing your debt? Consider the following:

Expressing our gratitude for where we are raises our energy level and therefore the energy level of the grid. Whenever we practice gratitude, we raise the energy around us like the ripples of a pond. Another way to raise energy? Work on your authentic self by tapping into that amazing heart of yours. We change the energy of the grid when we break out of a bad situation or change the rules. For example, if someone permanently gets out of a narcissistic relationship in business, a friendship, or romantic relationship that didn't make them happy, they have opened the grid and made it easier energetically for others to do the same. When I got out of my first marriage, women asked me how I found the courage to leave it. I used that opportunity to counsel others on how to have the courage to authentically step forward and claim what was true for us each individually, and together we raised the vibration of the grid.

Another example of opening the grid for others is illustrated by a friend of mine, Michelle, an engineering major in the early eighties. Not many women were in engineering then. In fact, Michelle's physics professor once confidently announced to the entire lecture hall that a woman (Michelle) got a 98 percent on the first exam and it would not happen again. Needless to say, it was a relatively hostile environment for women in that field. Even so, Michelle persisted and passed the class with a high grade. She and many more women before and after her opened up the grid to a point where now girls are encouraged to aspire to work in science, technology, engineering, and mathematics (STEM) careers.

When you make a positive change or open the grid for others, your ripple effect allows them to change for the better. This positive energy flow is the opposite of "misery loves company." It is an active, positive energy flow of change. It is the energy flow of love, like when the home team tends to win because the love of the fans fills the arena.

How do we tap into this energy of love? We awaken and jumpstart and revive the energy of the heart. An open and awakened heart means working from a state of peace where our passions, values, and purpose are aligned. It means you are aware of what you desire in your life. You know your values, and you know how to take responsibility for yourself and your emotions. We use this heart alignment to make more effective choices and actions to increase our real wealth.

How do we do that? We choose what makes us giggle and puts that smile on our face. Yes, it's all about finding your giggle! Imagine children lying in the grass thinking about what they are going to do today. They don't think of the past; they don't worry about what others think, and they certainly don't worry about the future. They live in the now, the present moment flowing from one thing to the next. What they do is not always logical, but it always makes them smile. They do what makes them happy or what makes them giggle. You need to be the same way!

You can drop into your heart-centered space by doing any of the following:

♡ Meditating

♡ Going outside

♡ Connecting with nature

♡ Making time for self-reflection

♡ Letting go of anything you're keeping out of obligation or guilt

♡ Following uplifting routines, such as taking a bubble bath or lifting weights

♡ Performing uplifting rituals, such as praying, dancing, or singing

♡ Taking a break

♡ Unplugging from technology to just "be"

♡ Having unstructured time on your calendar (my personal favorite)

♡ Doing the most self-loving thing in the moment, even if it ruffles some feathers

♡ And many more, create your own, I dare you ☺

When you align your actions and choices within your heart center, you are living in your truth, your authenticity. You are just being you, and you are speaking your truth. You are no longer giving up pieces of yourself to make others happy because you are not showing up as how your ego thinks other people expect. How other people react to you is their trigger not your trigger. You don't need to take it on. That is a choice. What do you choose? If you do something from your heart center and feel calm and happy with your decision, then you are in your authentic self. If someone else reacts with fear, anger, sadness, or the need to control, then there is something that needs to shift inside of them, not inside of you. Do not let them control you just so they feel more comfortable. Don't become hijacked or victimized by other people's issues. Don't show up for others in the way they want you to show up because then it's them just controlling you to obtain *their* desires. When you let others control you, you get trapped in your own nervous system and are no longer being authentic. It's not your truth, it's their truth. It can become an unending loop of personal suffering.

There are six control stress responses in our nervous system: fight, flight, control, disassociation, polarization (rigidity), or denial (putting our blinders on). If you feel any of these responses or if your body feels anxious or nervous when taking an action, this indicates that you have a trigger and need to pull out your toolbox of tricks to drop into your heart center and figure out your authentic truth. When we are not being authentic, we lose our freedom. Sometimes, your heart lets you know something is not working. Then you need to listen, admit it is not working, and decide to change. Choose to live life from a place of empowerment. **Be authentic, and stand in your truth. Live every day in alignment with your heart!**

When you live authentically, you elevate yourself, others, and the entire human energy grid. You have the courage to think outside of the box. The right path for you may not be the way others would do it, but you have no obligation to explain that method to anyone else. All that matters is just you and your heart. You can use your uniqueness to serve yourself and others. It may be in nontraditional ways. It may be the road less traveled or may not be the mainstream or popular path to take, but know you're being guided to do so. Sometimes, when we can get out of the forest of how other people say or do things, we see our own unique path. This is where creativity, innovation, and evolution are at peak performance—all because you followed your deep truth and chose to live authentically. That path is even better when we can serve ourselves and others with our unique, authentic self. When we are on this path to acquiring real wealth, we feel happy, calm, grounded, in the present moment, the now, and living in the natural flow of life. We can breathe deep here. Time flies because we are passionate about what we are doing.

Returning to Lisa, she searches out an opportunity to participate in a business panel at her local community college. It is aligned with her authentic goal of wanting to teach and the future she has envisioned for herself. She uses her business knowledge to walk across the bridge over to the career she wants to embrace. She took action to seek out this opportunity.

Let's see how else intention redirects our energy with the next law.

CHAPTER 3

*"Every journey begins with the first step
of articulating the intention, and then
becoming the intention."*

—BRYANT MCGILL

As YOU CLIMB onto the next step of your journey, let's consider the third Spiritual Law of Money: **Intention redirects energy.** We are going to talk about changing your energy flow by using your intentions. You have the picture of what you want to manifest, and you have explored your authenticity, taken stock of your present situation, and awakened your heart. To make a positive change in the energy grid, you must raise your vibration. Use your intentions as a power tool to shift your energy, and a positive change will occur right before your eyes. All the synchronicities of life will line up even better than before. You also can see them more clearly now that you've set your intentions. Your radar, or awareness, is on the lookout. Remember that your energy flows where your intention goes. Setting your intention to change isn't always easy, and sometimes we need to practice to move in the right direction. As a reminder, it's like building a muscle—a financial muscle.

As part of awakening your heart, you realized that you need to change to manifest your dreams. In the last chapter, you made a heart-centered examination of where you are. You examined your current situation and accepted all the good and bad in it. You understand that you need an intention to change and as a part of that intention, you must have the personal power and energy for the change. To consolidate and gain enough of your personal power to set your intention and change the course of your energy stream, you must clear away the things that no longer work for you. This could be repeating the financial pattern of spending when you are feeling down, hoarding things "just in case" something happens, using retail therapy to keep your ego buzz going, or staying in a job that you have outgrown and that no longer excites you. Find the courage to take a hard look at the things, patterns, or people who are not helping you reach your next apex, or summit of your life, and remove them from your current reality to create a whole new world for yourself. If you resist dealing with these issues, they will persist in showing up. When you put up with things, situations, or people who aren't in alignment with your true self, you're energetically telling the world, the universe, and God, that you want more of the status quo, which you know is not your truth.

Another way to say this is that everyone plays roles. This has everything to do with how you see and portray yourself. We train people how to treat us. Whether you are the victim, martyr, hero, child, giver, taker, provider for others, rich, or poor. These roles tend to stick, and we become them. Throw away the roles you used in the past to get things, when you were in survival mode, as they no longer serve you. You can't gain your personal power if you and others see you as the victim, because the victim has no power. You are required to stop playing the blame game. A business mentor and dear friend of mine, Bob Lyman, taught me something years ago when I was in my twenties. He would say, "Murph, you know, when you point the finger at someone or something else as the cause of what has happened in your life, take a look at the direction of your other three fingers on that hand."

Try it, for yourself, right now. Point your finger, and observe which direction your middle, ring, and pinky finger are pointing. Yep, you guessed it. They are pointing right back at you. Blame is how we deflect looking at what is not in alignment with us on the inside. So, if you blame anyone and everyone but yourself, the next time something bad happens, ask yourself, "What is coming up within me that needs to be addressed or healed?" When you choose not to blame any longer, you take the responsibility for your life. This is the act of choosing your life from a place of empowerment, not by coasting away by default. The one common denominator in all your problems and joy in your life is you. You are the creator of your life. When we stop repeating our sad and traumatic stories, sit with the feelings and let them pass through us, this enables us to break through. The only way through the tough times is to feel them, acknowledge them, and accept that they are hard. Say, "Yes, that did happen, and yes, that is my reality."

What would this change do for your current situation and the acquiring of your dream vision? If you choose to see a different perspective, your reality will change. You'll be amazed at what you see once you open yourself up to truly look. The less you are willing to adjust or change, the longer it will take to align your lifestyle to your new vision. Life has a way of continuing to teach you the lessons with different names and faces, but the same patterns reoccur until you shift your pattern. You have to believe that you have other options.

Set the intention to *see* those other options and then ask to be shown them with ease and grace. Interestingly enough, often we are not given many options. Usually, people only see two of them. Sometimes, they only see two undesirable choices. This is your test to either go back to the old or jump into the new. When that happens to you, look out of the box (of the obvious choices) to come up with another unique or unconventional choice. Sometimes, the choice is not clear, but we just know it's not a "yes" yet. Trust that things take time to align. I always remind myself that "divine timing is not Julie timing." Remember to look out for anyone trying to put limits on you. Or choose to take a minimally viable choice. The minimally viable choice is not a whole step into one of your undesirable choices, but it is a baby step. Take one small action toward your vision. Trust your gut! Often, you know you want to move forward, you just don't quite see how the puzzle fits together. Trust all will be good, and in time the pattern will make sense.

Let me give you an example from my own life. Years ago, just after the birth of my fourth child, I was given the opportunity to take my kids on vacation—by myself. At the time, I really didn't see it as an opportunity. Honestly, I was quite ticked off about it, but something told me to go regardless of the new circumstances. I wondered, *how in the heck am I going to drive, by myself, for six hours up to northern Michigan with four kids under the age of six?* Well, we did it! It took eight hours for the ride due to the many pit stops, but we had a great week to ourselves up there. Little did I know that I was being prepped to learn how to manage four kids all by myself because not even a year later, I was divorced. I was building the muscle to take care of my kids by myself and run a company at the same time. Divine orchestration for sure! Sometimes, taking one small step opens up other opportunities and allows you to take another better step. Other times, it allows you to clear your vision and see where you should have gone. It's all information guiding you to the next right step.

Lisa knows that to achieve her vision she has to change; something has got to give. Right now, she thinks that she only has the choice to remain in the job that no longer serves her or to take a job teaching a community college class. If she takes the community college job, she will also take a huge pay cut. She doesn't like either alternative. The situation doesn't have to be an "either or." It can be an "and." So, Lisa sets the intention to manifest her dream. She decides to take a minimally viable choice to teach an evening class at the community college. This allows her to see if she likes teaching in a small classroom. It also enables her to gain experience teaching so she could get a better job at this college or at a bigger university. Like Lisa, allow yourself to be on the bridge between point A and point B. Allow your dream the time it needs to unfold.

Your words can shape your reality or limit your possibilities. Be aware of the language that you use. We often communicate from a place of scarcity or victimhood. "There is not enough of [X] . . ." or "I could never accomplish that because [Y] . . .". We keep hitting the edit button and judging things before we give them a shot! Be loving and considerate of your feelings and needs in your self-talk because *you* matter. Anger and hate don't leave you any room for change or understanding let alone the cortisol that it shoots through your veins, creating health issues over time. The words we use, as well as how we treat others, ourselves, and our surroundings, all contribute to our well-being. If you don't react positively to someone or people don't bring out the best in you, stop spending time with them.

Often, we don't feel this is a choice, but it is.

I worked with a person who spent their career breaking down glass ceilings from prior generations in their field of study. Remember when I said you'll continue to attract those who have the same patterning unless you do your work to heal your childhood rejection or trauma that occurred before the age of seven? Well, this person was no different. He had done tons of work on healing from his childhood with a narcissistic parent. On the surface, all seemed like it was headed in the healthiest direction possible. Little did he know that the employer he chose was led by the narcissist of narcissists.

The president of the corporation was a textbook narcissist, just like this person's parent. Clearly, he had some unresolved healing to do or else this employer would not have impacted him like they did. He was put to the ultimate test. He worked hard for a number of years, completely turned his division around, and just when he was supposed to get huge long-term incentive payouts, the rug was pulled out from underneath him. Instead, his company handed him a severance package. Of course, they did not offer him what he deserved. So, he put together a response validating the reasons for a better severance package only to be shut down and told, "Take what we offered or leave it." Wow, the power play was on. He was not sure about what next step to take. I told him, "Well, do you want to play with a narcissist again? They love the fight. Do you want to fight? Or do you just want to spend your energy creating the next phase of your life on your terms?"

I've helped many people, including myself, reach business deals or divorce settlements that most financial professionals would completely disagree with because they weren't "fair." Define fair. To me, it's all about considering what energy you want to be in. Do you want to be in a two- to three-year divorce fight and have it suck the life out of you? Or do you want to settle out with something you can reasonably live with so you can just move on with your life? Define how one gets the short end of the stick. People tell me I was a fool for settling out how I did with my divorce. However, I chose every ounce of it from a place of empowerment. It took eleven months to get divorced and that was even too long, but I settled out. I knew I would grow immensely after the divorce was final, and my company and I have. It just keeps getting better. This is how the energy behind everything works. Whatever you speak, think, and feel is what will become. Choose your words, thoughts, and feelings wisely. Don't let the memories of what others have said in your past define who you are today or shape your tomorrow. Decide to let go of a ten-second memory to lighten your load from your past. Life is much easier when you do.

What is holding you back? What beliefs define your behavior? If you reframe the negative, you can create a positive movement in your life. Positive thoughts expressed with positive words and feelings create—you guessed it—a positive reality!

Changing years and years of patterns of less-than-optimal choices is not easy. Those grooves are deep in your brain. Give yourself time to shift the patterns. Loving and treating yourself with grace will make this transition easier. Remember, you are worth it. The world needs you and your authentic gifts. By applying practical and simple techniques when setting your intentions and taking small, positive steps, you can make huge forward strides. Life is about choices. Your life is an amalgamation of these choices. If you need a little help in this area, check out this exercise.

 EXERCISE TIME – LET'S BUILD THOSE MUSCLES
Cleaning Out Old Patterns

Think of cleansing away everything you dislike about your current situation like cleaning out the refrigerator—remove the old to make room for the new. Close your eyes, and let your mind explore the possibilities of releasing each of these items. Then complete "I choose to _____" with your newly chosen behaviors. Here are a few examples:

- ♡ I choose to live within my means.
- ♡ I choose to face my current financial reality.
- ♡ I choose work that is in alignment with my soul and how I want to be of service in the world.
- ♡ I choose to nurture treasured relationships with my family.
- ♡ I choose to spend time with someone who loves and values me, a true partner.

Or state your intentions:

- ♡ I choose to save $100 a month for six months.
- ♡ I choose to have a positive relationship with money.
- ♡ I choose to have wealth in abundance.
- ♡ I choose to release all patterns of scarcity.
- ♡ I choose to proactively reduce my financial past and debt balances.
- ♡ I choose to log my health progress daily to become more aware of my nutritional choices.
- ♡ I choose to love myself enough to release excess weight to be healthier.
- ♡ I choose to take at least 10,000 steps a day.
- ♡ I choose to update my resume and share it with the world.

The possibilities are endless because they are yours. We live in a quantum field of infinite opportunities. Carefully read through your list, then rewrite statements on sticky notes and plaster them all over your home as a constant reminder of how you choose to live. Repeat them throughout your day with the assumption that they have already happened. Before long, these conscious choices will become your "clear intent," creating new behaviors and a new reality.

Practicing this Spiritual Law, **intention redirects energy**, is the pivot point from examining your *spiritual* aspect, your vision, your current reality, and your acceptance of the need to change, to your *physical* aspect of setting your intention to change and take action. As stated before, if you feel grounded in your decision, it aligns with your heart and soul. If you experience anxiety or depression in your decision to move forward, then your vision came from just your ego and your mind and is probably not authentic and true to your heart. When you choose to follow your ego and mind, it's not about what you internally want; making this choice leads to not having sustainable happiness, joy, and satisfaction with a life well lived. These thoughts come from an external perception, like the ego thinking you need to keep up with the Joneses or live up to someone else's expectation. In our example, Lisa's case, societal expectations say that all businesspeople should strive and want to be at the executive level. I ask this: At what cost?

Trauma or rejection in our younger years conditioned us not to trust our hearts. This rejection or trauma causes us not to trust our knowing. This is one thing that no longer serves us and that we need to get rid of. To release these feelings from rejection or trauma, examine them closely. Go ahead and feel those feelings and acknowledge that they are valid. If you're like me, I was so detached that I had to ask myself why I was angry, which is deep sadness, and why those feelings continually came up and out. The only way to get on the other side of this stormy sea of emotions is through it. Another huge clue that you are not connected to your higher self? When you try to people-please, by overworking or using black-and-white thinking. When you people-please by not setting personal boundaries, you give your power to someone else, all in the name of "I was just trying to help" or some other phrase that justifies our lack of self-love. You are not being authentic to who you are.

I am not saying that you have to be mean or selfish to be authentic, but we have all done something for a friend that we really didn't want to do, such as allowing them to duck their responsibilities or bailing them out of a bad situation. Is this being a good friend? Is it optimal if you don't show up in the best version of you, the way you were made to positively impact the world? Sometimes when we bail others out, they don't get the opportunity to become aware of what they've created in their lives, and so, they don't rise to a realization of how to make different, better life choices. Is that optimal? Doing something helpful for someone once in a while is being a good friend. When you do it constantly, to gain the feeling of acceptance, it can drain your energy to the point that none remains for what you need to accomplish. I know because I've lived it.

A great example of this is work. Many times, we, especially women, feel we need to be grateful to have a job. We think that we have no choice but to take everything that work hands out, good or bad. We're often just happy to be at the table. From a personal or an employee point of view, we don't always get what we need. Oftentimes, we never even address these needs, whether they are a raise, better software, or flexible hours. Part of taking responsibility for your life is realizing your worth. Yes, you are lucky to have a job, but on the other side of the coin, your employer is lucky to have *you*. Feel free to negotiate for what you want and need. The worst that will happen is that they will say no. If they do, ask them for a plan of action so that you can work toward that plan, execute it, and hold them accountable to following through with their promises. Or, call their bluff and choose another path that is healthier for you financially, personally, and professionally. Remember, negotiation is standing up for yourself, but it is also your willingness to listen to the other side and potentially compromise on a reasonable solution for both parties.

You and your employer are partners, not grateful servant and master. The servant and master setup is a win/lose game that you'll never win in the long run, even if in the short run they've pacified you. But how many of us operate in the grateful servant and master dynamic because we need our paychecks to pay for all of our debts and responsibilities? I would love for us all to get to a place where we *want* our jobs but don't *need* our jobs. That shifts us from victim and scarcity mode to empowered and abundance mode. If your situation is sucking away your soul and your employer is not willing to negotiate to make it better, Source may be telling you that you have learned what you need to from that job and it is time to move on. If you choose not to move forward, eventually the opportunity of you leaving will be the choice of your employer because of the energetic mismatch and Source nudging you along. I see this all the time. For years, people give all their blood, sweat, and tears at the cost of living a life they love, only to be dropped like a hot potato in an instant by their employer. We can completely avoid this if we listen to our hearts and trust that the paycheck will follow.

You are at your highest vibration or the apex of your authenticity when you align your thoughts with your feelings. When you are your authentic self, you are at your most powerful. Do you know that brain cells are in our hearts? Yep, it's true! When we activate these cells, they connect to the brain cells in our mind, and this leads to the magic of what scientists call coherence. It is time that you change your outlook and center to a more positive language.

Let's look at an example. You may want a relationship that you don't currently have. Instead of thinking that no one wants you, map out what you desire in a partner while you are working on making yourself whole. The next exercise works on reframing your negatives into positives.

 **EXERCISE TIME — LET'S BUILD THOSE MUSCLES**
Turn Your Negatives into Positives

Write down the things you would like to do but feel you'll never have sufficient money or time to make happen. Don't be shy. Don't edit yourself. By all means, do not negotiate yourself away. Allow the magic to work in your favor. Next to each item, write the specific reason you think it can't or won't work. For example, in my twenties, I was starting a business, cash flow was always tight, and I still had lots of debt from putting myself through college. I wanted to visit Ireland, where my family is from, but I had no clue how to make that happen. I just decided that, somehow, I was going to Ireland, and I shifted how I spoke about it. This attitude began to open up possibilities. Being one of twelve children, I never thought I would ever travel to Wisconsin let alone to another country. The odds were stacked against me. Wouldn't you know, within a year of shifting how I perceived my outcomes and talking about how I was going to go to Ireland, the opportunity came to me. A friend asked me if I wanted to run the Dublin Marathon. Well, for those of you who know me, I am not a runner. An athlete yes, but I've never been a long-distance runner. I was told that if I raised $2,400 for the Arthritis Foundation, my airfare, hotel, and entry into the Dublin Marathon would be covered. And for an extra $1,000, I could bring a guest. I agreed to the offer. Raising funds for charity was supernatural since I went to a Catholic school, which we raised money for all the time. I knew how to do this, and I did. It's funny how life turns out. By the way, I took Mom to Ireland with me as my guest.

Now, it's your turn. Please, love yourself enough to detach from "how" it will all show up. Your job is to have a clear intention of what you want to create in your life and to align your thoughts, feelings, and words with that outcome. Now, I'd like you to revisit each reason you've listed and reframe each to be more positive, using affirmative language. Write down something actionable. Life is too short to waste time with negativity. Focus on "can" instead of "can't" and "will" instead of "won't." That way, you'll be a lot closer to living your authentic life.

Can't	Can
Want	Like/Desire/Wish
Should	Would/Could/Can
Try	Do
Hope	Trust
No More Buts	Use "and"
No Fault or Blame	Take Responsibility

Consider these examples of negatives reframed as positives:

I can't leave my job.	I can be happy in my career and get paid what I deserve.
I want a bigger house.	I desire to buy my dream home.
I should stop using my credit cards.	I can get what I want using the cash that I have.
I should try to stop spending.	I do want financial peace in my life.
I hope I'll be able to retire one day.	I trust I will retire comfortably.
I could stop giving money to my kids, but . . .	I can help my kids out and teach them fiscal responsibility.
I'd have more money if they stopped raising taxes (blame).	I can use creative tax strategies to reduce taxes owed (take responsibility).

As we have talked about, what you do, say, and feel matter vibrationally. You are trying to raise your vibration to pull into your vision of the future. Life is like a river. The flowing water from the past has led us to where we are today. We need to live today while paying for, or cleaning up, the decisions we made yesterday. You can't go back and recapture that stream runoff. You must release your old memories and behaviors and look at today. As a river flows, just like water does, it takes the path of least resistance. When this happens to you, know it is where your heart is. It's where time flies by and you wonder how it went so fast. It's because you are in the flow of life, the present moment, the now, with your heart along for the ride.

The river is constantly moving and flowing, and we consciously need to pay attention to our present moment. Look at it like a child seeing something for the very first time. Children's thoughts and dreams are unlimited. If you choose to observe and accept your current situation, you won't pull your past into your present, which creates your past again as your future. You must unlock yourself from the prison of this past and continue down the river. Choose the path of least resistance. Go into the flow of life, and when more arises that triggers you, observe it, feel it, accept it, and just keep flowing.

Your financial story is written in your accounts of debt, your cash inflows and outflows, and your assets. If you are in debt, set up automatic payments to pay down that debt. Don't give it any more attention once the setup is complete. If you keep focusing on your debt, you are only going to create more of it. Spend your energy and attention on what you want to create in your life with the money left over. But it is also good practice to set up automatic transfers to your savings accounts so you don't have to concentrate on growing your money either. All the time, clients tell me, "Wow, I didn't realize there was that much in my account now." It's on autopilot, and they are just living life and all their desires are being funded just like an automatic deposit of your paycheck to your checking account. You can use this system to your advantage to create a life that you love, one deposit at a time. This leaves you more energy to create your vision of the future.

Everything is vibrational—words, thoughts, feelings, and actions. That is why you want to have gratitude for what you have and the insights you're getting. Choosing to stay open allows you to be in the mystery of the now and of how your future will be created. You won't see how your dream will manifest, but you will know it is all aligned. You are putting your thoughts, words, feelings, and energy into what you want to happen. What you do now matters vibrationally. Where we are today will be our past in the future. What you choose to change today will help you create your future. When you follow your heart and soul, you will also get to a place where you don't desire any more material things because you won't get the fake ego buzz of ownership. You will yearn for life experiences over material objects. Your ego wants the material goods to show status and to keep up with the Joneses. You'll say goodbye to all that. Who are the Joneses anyway? But, by choosing your heart-centered focus, you can find your happiness now. You can never replace today, so why not be happy? Just open up to receive. Living in the now allows this to happen. The happiness you are building is built on a solid foundation, not on wobbly ego stilts. Now that you have chosen to change, it's time to take action.

CHAPTER 4

*"If you don't go after what you want,
you'll never have it. If you don't ask,
the answer is always no. If you don't step forward,
you're always in the same place."*

—NORA ROBERTS

THE FOURTH SPIRITUAL Law of Money, **the universe responds to action**, is about stepping forward in your journey to make your manifestation a reality. Up to now, we have tackled our spiritual, intellectual, and emotional selves. Now, we must bring those plans into the physical realm and make them tangible. So many people meditate and receive messages, but they don't take any action to seed those intentions for their lives. Once you plant the seed of possibility (your manifestation), you have to water, weed, and cultivate it. It won't grow and thrive without this action. You must invest your energy into it. Your action is your skin in the game called life.

Sometimes, we procrastinate. Sometimes, a limiting belief that we "can't" do something prevents us from getting started. But since we have aligned our heads with our hearts, we know that we now can move forward. Even if it is the minimal viable choice, a baby step, it's still a step forward. Go at whatever pace you want, slow or fast. Just keep moving forward. Most often, people find their happiness from a sense of accomplishment, comparing where they are today versus yesterday. Even a small step forward is progress. It's a win! And, it has nothing to do with anyone else. All that matters is that you're moving in the direction of your heart and soul. The more you do this, things start to shift faster and bigger leaps come, moving you forward to your new reality. Speaking of wins, don't forget to reward yourself when you reach an important milestone or goal. This allows you to feel a sense of accomplishment and happiness, which helps you keep going and following the path that is meant for you.

With the past Spiritual Laws, we have integrated our heads (intellectual) and our hearts (spiritual and emotional). Now, we are going to integrate the fourth piece of our being: the physical. In your physical past, your actions may have been predominantly driven by your masculine energy, where you pushed, competed, blocked, tackled, and plowed forward to get your way. The challenge here? You only have so much capacity. You probably had a huge to-do list that you were either compelled to complete or pushed to the background to procrastinate about. Now, it is time for a different approach. Let your to-do list become secondary. Work from your feminine energy, where you are following your intuition, following your inner knowing, allowing things space to rise to the occasion, accepting all that arises in your life, being, and going with the flow just like a river. It's the pull energy, attracting the things you want, versus the push energy, which is the blocking, tackling, and doing to make things happen.

What is the flow? It's the allowing of things to unfold. It takes patience. I know, this is not easy for some of us Type A personalities! The flow is when you drop into your heart center, feel connected, and allow that to direct your life. Psychologist Mihaly Csikszentmihalyi described "being in the flow" as experiencing a feeling of timelessness, where tasks seem easy and things just "come together." Csikszentmihalyi described the state of flow as enjoyable. The amount of effort and loss of time don't matter, just like those kids during summer break implementing their great plans. When you are in the flow, your journey will be easier. It's the absence of resistance. If what you do to act upon your desires takes a huge amount of hard pushing, you are not in your flow and maybe you are not meant to do what you are doing. Experiencing peak flow requires active participation in the real physical world. You must take action. When you act, if you are mindful about it (aligned with your intention and heart), the universe responds and enables you to easily travel your correct path. It's about moving forward as the synchronicities of life align due to the first three Spiritual Laws of Money. But you have to direct your energy in the direction of your flow. Meaning as things arise, or align, in your flow, you need to participate and step forward into the direction you desire your life to go. It'll never happen unless you do. Participating is your skin in the game of life, your life. If you want to hear more about being in the flow, check out Adam Grant's talk "How to Stop Languishing and Start Finding Flow" on TED.com.

Sometimes, fear prevents us from being in the flow, and it shows up as resistance. If you operate from a place of fear and panic (lodged in your ego mind and not in your heart), you can't create what you desire. Fear holds the bonds and limits of the unknown and suffering in place. You operate from a viewpoint of survival instead of thriving and abundance. You need to feel safe in your heart center. When you feel safe, you open up to your flow. You open up to receive money, love, happiness, joy, and much more. So, whatever feels safe for you, whether that is fast or slow, go at your safe pace. Safety is the key. This is where you meet yourself where you are. Right or wrong does not exist; neither does good or bad. It's just what feels safe.

When we feel safe, we can expand. When we don't feel safe, our lives contract and we build walls until we feel safe again. These walls block the flow of life and block things showing up in our lives, from money, to relationships, to the ideal job, etc. Of course, if you are in the flow, you may find that your journey is timeless and you are moving faster

than you thought possible. This is where quantum leaps occur. However, don't confuse fear with a little bit of nervous excitement. Fear stops you from moving forward, but it is perfectly acceptable to feel a few butterflies as you step into the unknown of manifesting your desires.

For example, I am currently working on health and wellness. When my body is jammed up with toxins, it's hard to follow my body's intelligence. As I mentioned earlier, your body houses your intuition, which sends more messages to your brain than your nervous system does. If you are eating fruit and vegetables and exercising, you are a much clearer channel and can access those flow messages faster. It's time for us to realize how this is all connected. For years, I always knew I needed to lose weight. The realization that I was blocking my heart's desires from manifesting because I couldn't manage my diet effectively long-term became my compelling reason for change. No way was I going to keep allowing my childhood trauma to activate my automatic response system to stress eat. Eating was my coping mechanism. So, I dealt with trauma head-on, shifted all kinds of people and patterns I held for years, and now the weight is melting off. For good! Why? Because now I feel safe. My younger self had hardwired into my subconscious mind that if I didn't feel safe, I'd eat to return me to a place of safety. This cycle kept going on and on and on. Exhausting! Therefore, I decided to stop this cycle dead in its tracks.

Don't be afraid of going against "everyone else's" flow. If a financial planner tells you that you can't afford to take a vacation, but your heart, intelligence, emotions, and spirit say you need a break for your own safety, what do you do? Remember, it's an "and" not an "or." So, while your financial planner is saying that due to the way you normally spend, you shouldn't take that vacation, instead of not going, try another approach—one where you plan to go on vacation but figure out where the funds will come from without creating debt. This could be another spending account or emergency reserves, if it's available. Remember, your well-being is no longer negotiable. Pay attention to your knowing, and take a vacation. That doesn't mean you shouldn't search for bargain accommodations. Create and stick to a travel budget.

Consider this example from my divorce: I incurred debt in the process of the marital split—debt that made me feel unsafe. So, I went against traditional financial wisdom and took money out of my kids' college funds to pay it off. Wow, with that burden gone, I could focus more on expanding in business and writing this book. I no longer experienced the energy of stress and strain on cash flows. A dark force lifted off of me, and I was free to fly again. Moving out of that energy helped me establish my new flow. Later, I was able to replace this money from a better place.

Another place where I see people going against their flows and intentions? When they buy financial products. So many people buy whatever products their financial advisor, family, friends, or coworkers recommend. You should align your products with your personal strategy. Today's typical financial services professional looks at banking, risk management, and investing as a black-and-white discipline, logically and statistically focused. They are not looking at your heart center or holistically at your life. They are also not identifying if it is the smart financial thing to do for *you* and/or if it is the direction that you want to go. It's important to fund who you are and what is also going to optimize returns where you feel safe. You're bringing you along into the picture. The whole you— right brain and left brain, and most importantly, your heart!

Remember Michelle, from physics – the one who endured a hostile academic environment? She is fifty-seven now, maybe closer to retirement than you. Her retirement financial statement always shows that she is at a much higher risk factor than her age group. She invests in startups (mostly tech), and startups are high risk. These investments make her feel alive and invigorated because they have purpose and meaning to her. Along with this, she's also chosen to only put 15 percent of her assets in the bucket. Why? Because she is close to retirement and wants the rest of her money spread out to lower risking investments. As the riskier ones grow or lose, she considers, with intention, what to do with the gains and how to rebalance often unexpected losses. The key? She does all of this with intention and awareness, fueled by her personal strategy. She enjoys her work immensely and can work anywhere, so she doesn't see herself retiring anytime soon. Taking some risk makes her feel safe—comfortable.

Now, take that first safe step, whether it is putting your credit cards in the freezer, investing in companies you personally align with based on your values, eating berries instead of a huge piece of chocolate cake, or no longer spending time with those who keep you stuck by reinforcing your old patterns. Once you step into where you are aligned with your heart, the hooks that kept you hanging will fall away and you can move forward. Your focus will shift to intentional creation instead of emotional reaction. All the things we have talked about from this point will have built you up to where you can execute in the flow. I come from a profession where people only execute, and sometimes that is hard because you haven't taken the time to align with your heart. Be aware about why you are doing some things and not doing others. The path should always be clear in the direction of your heart's desire.

So many people feel that money is everything—that "once I have this much money, it will all be okay." This couldn't be further from the truth. When you get that much money, something else comes up and then you need more. The cycle never ends. It's about shifting your financial patterns. Since your energy is tied up into getting "enough" money, you create a never-ending hamster wheel of suffering to reach an "I am enough" or "I am worthy" destination that never arrives. It's a pattern that you can absolutely break.

For some reason, our collective culture pursues the narrative that not having a "high income" means you can't have a high quality of life. This notion is not necessarily true. Yes, having more money is nice, and it can give you more material choices, but it's not the whole picture. What is more important is what you do with the income you have. I've seen people who make $40,000 annually who are way happier than those who make $600,000 annually. It's about directing your cash inflow intentionally and choosing cash outflows that are your priority, not by default. This is a personal choice. It gives you more freedom and the power to create the quality of life you desire. This puts you in the power seat. It's taking the steering wheel of your life and turning it in any direction you want. Sometimes, this takes creative solutions, but know there is always a way.

How do you break that "enough money" pattern? The more detached you are from the final outcome of money, the more of it you will attract. When you detach from the monetary importance, you create more energy and this allows for expansion in your life. Your job is to create and hold that space while taking actionable steps.

You may be surprised that your money issues are not strangling you while you are holding this space for potential. You have no idea what your potential is, but your job is to detach from how you arrive at the outcome and stay curious along your journey. Whatever is meant for you—money, relationships, your health, or work—can't miss you. It is drawn into that space from where you set your intention. It gives you so much freedom. One woman told me, as she was redesigning her life, "I sold my house, and I bought my freedom."

This home was in an expensive city and cost more than she had ever paid for a house before. To afford it, she had to keep performing at high levels at work. What she once loved, the object of a longtime dream, became a burden. As she suffered under its weight, she realized that she placed a higher value on freedom to travel and spending time with loved ones than on a material object, this home.

Everything started to unravel for this woman when, at fifty-eight years old, she was let go from her job. It was the best gift she ever received. She spent the next decade traveling. Each year, she spent three months living in Seattle, where she sold her home, three months in London with a friend, three months in Arizona, and three months in her birth city, visiting family in sweet home Chicago! She was reinvigorated like she couldn't ever have imagined, filled with lots of love, laughter, freedom, happiness, and joy! She was also able to spend four months living with her mom before her mom left this earthly plane. What a priceless gift, all because she got fired and chose her freedom over continuing to create more suffering patterns. We need to realize that our life direction is a choice we *all* can make. It's about doing what makes you happy and what you love, otherwise on some level you won't feel safe. When we don't feel safe, things start to deteriorate. Creating a safe container to be exactly who you are all of the time is very important.

To hold that potential space, often you have to set boundaries. You may have to let go of some ideas, patterns, or people that prohibit you from reaching your utmost potential, regardless of the temporary impact on your bank account. It's just a transition, and change often makes us feel uncomfortable as we find our legs to step into the new. This is using the detachment from money that we just discussed. Just trust that all will align and be provided for, even though you may not know "how" it will all show up. Let's look at an example:

I had a very difficult client—a high-dollar client who wanted to control things in a way that prohibited my team from doing our job. Through the years, we watched her feeling unhappy with her emergency reserves, guys she dated, and family members, and eventually we made it to her chopping block as well. She communicated that she was not happy with us and listed her reasons why. I came to realize that she was breaking my boundaries of client relations and taking up way too much of my and my staff's time and energy without reasonable compensation. Her emails illustrated all the areas where she was trying to control everything and everyone. It became exhausting. No one wanted to take her calls. Once I realized this, the final email came. At that moment, I chose to release her by finding her a financial planner who would be a better fit. I worried a little about my bottom line as this client had millions, but she was much happier with her new financial planner. My team and I were just as happy.

So, how does the energetic world work with a situation like this? I immediately set my intention that I wanted to call in more clients, like another woman who was just a joy to work with. We managed even more money for this woman. She always expressed gratitude, let us do what we do best, and trusted the process in working with our team. I wasn't sure exactly how filling the void of losing a client would show up, but I knew that if I held the intention of what I wanted to create, because we are the creators of our lives, somehow, things would appear. They did. I was super excited when this amazing client brought in three referrals, which I now had more time for. These new referrals had more assets for us to manage and took less time to work with because they too trusted the process and allowed us to do our jobs. They spoke to us with respect and were just kind human beings and so pleasant to deal with. So, I increased my accounts by setting healthy boundaries for me and my team after detaching from money and letting go of a client I was no longer aligned with. Why do we think this is bad? It's okay to release what no longer serves us. I realized that the gift that client brought me was to establish healthy boundaries no matter what—and that all can still work out perfectly.

Notice that I reaffirmed my boundaries in a loving way. I didn't just dump the client and tell her to get out. No, I referred her to a new place to get her needs met. I even followed up with her to find out if she was in a better place than when I left her. You can protect your boundaries with love and without giving into fear that someone will take advantage of you.

Managing your real wealth is not a one and done thing. Managing real wealth requires you to understand yourself at deeper and deeper levels each time. It is like peeling an onion a layer at a time. Like an onion, where you are reaching toward your inner core, you are reaching to the deepest core of your being and true self. Unlike the onion, however, you are expanding your expression in the world. So, as this expansion happens, you have to think about the legacy you want to leave behind. What imprint do you want to leave on the world? What impact or difference do you want to make?

You are putting your energetic spark out into the world. The more regularly and consistently you take practical action to manifest your desires about your real wealth, the more effective your outcomes will be. Think of yourself as an energetic vortex. Let me give you a visual. See it as the opposite of a tornado yet similar in shape. Instead of creating destruction like a tornado does, think of it as powerful, a swirl of energy that keeps getting bigger and bigger. The more it swirls, collecting all that comes through its path, the more and more impact it makes. As it swirls, it tosses away all that doesn't help it grow and expand. It continues to move forward and can reach extreme forces of energy. It becomes a force to be reckoned with, and so can you.

You can be a positive energetic force in the world that doesn't allow anything to stop it from your soul's path. The universe responds to action. You can dream and set intentions all you want, but if you don't use practical action steps as the synchronicities of life start to appear, you won't become a strong vortex of real wealth. It is your signal to the universe that you are constant and true. You are claiming who and what you are and not apologizing for it. You are fully embodying your greatness, living in your truth and your authenticity, creating deep happiness and soulful satisfaction and contentment of a life you are living. The money that comes to you is just a result of your alignment with you. Now, it is not always easy to stay that consistent, but remember that even small, consistent steps are moving you forward. You don't have to go rogue and jump off a cliff. It's okay to take one step at a time to cross that bridge. Just do what makes you feel grounded yet excited at the same time.

You can help yourself by having a monthly financial date night with your significant other, a friend, a mentor, or with yourself. Look over your finances. Pay attention to your spending and incoming assets and tweak your cash outflows for any expenditures that are on the horizon. Take a look at your savings and give yourself credit for the progress you have made. Also, look at your personal, spiritual, family, and career conditions and your dreams and goals. Make sure you and your partner discuss each other's thoughts on how these things are going.

In addition, make a dream list and write down the things you've always wanted to do that haven't occurred yet—the things that you are excited about. During financial date night, once every quarter, look at what you have accomplished on the list. Tune into your heart, and ask yourself if the things left open are still important. If they are, keep them on the list. If not, take them off. Also ask if there is anything you are passionate about adding. You must be as consistent as you can with your finances and other aspects of your life, and you have to put a little energy into them. It's like a relationship. You need to invest time and put some attention toward it, or it can go off track.

As I expressed in *Awaken Your Wealth,* there are different classifications of people who are dealing with money. The first category we are going to talk about are the Debtors—a hybrid of people who have access to some credit but are of the scarcity mindset. At this stage of the game, Debtors are managing their wealth by robbing Peter to pay Paul. They come from the energy of lack, where there is not enough. It makes them constantly juggle their finances because they don't have enough assets to cover their expenses. Because of the juggling, they lack the freedom or the energy to hold any potential to make change.

So many people today live a higher lifestyle but have achieved it by accumulating debt, which traps them. They have limited their choices in their job and reduced their power to live their dreams because they are spending faster than their earning capability. Their cash flow deposited into their checking account from their employers is going to pay for all of their past debt decisions, making it incredibly challenging to live in the present moment. They live on a shaky foundation built on stilts instead of firm financial decisions. Their foundation is not firm enough to launch them into their desired life. The banks and their debtors run their life, not them. They're living, working, eating, and breathing to keep the bank alive instead of themselves. They have given their personal power away to the banks and their employers. Their life is no longer their own.

The group known as Dreamers is a blend of scarcity and abundance. I refer to this blend as the hybrid model. They go in and out of scarcity and abundance. Scarcity, because they don't believe there is enough and they have given their personal power away to others like their debtors, the banks, and their employer; and abundance because they have gotten pretty good at cash flow management and their debt levels come down, but then they tend to go back up again to truly break those subconscious money patterns they learned in the households and communities in which they grew up. They are starting to realize that they can do things, but they don't have any idea about how to get there and they have yet to take any action. But they are excited and ready for a change. They are ready to try anything to get to the other side. This is why they're called Dreamers. If they looked at their heart center and took action consistently and regularly, they could open their energy enough to their potential. However, they never *quite* get there and are in a perpetual state of limbo, a teeter-totter of sorts.

Accumulators, in turn, move in and out of financial scarcity and abundance, but they tend to be on the higher side of the abundance scale because, most of the time, they usually live within their means. Accumulators live in the current moment. Their debt is considered good debt (mortgage, student loans, etc.), which is misleading because any debt is a state of a lack of freedom today due to cash inflows having to pay for past choices. They live more in the present moment because they have more income affluence, and since they have less debt, they can spend more in cash outlays. They are considered income affluent, but not yet asset affluent, meaning their income allows them to live a lifestyle they desire, but they have not accumulated enough assets to be financially independent to stop working and retire to maintain their current lifestyle. Their foundation is still shaky because their house foundation is not aligned with their heart center.

Many have created their income affluence in careers that don't fully feed their heart and soul. Their jobs fed their heart and soul at one time, but today it does not, which is a sign to step into the next adventure. Once they become asset affluent as well, they will realize that they still don't feel any different because they will lack deep happiness, joy, and contentment for the life they are living. This is where money can leak out by way of divorce, unplanned severance from work, an unexpected health issue arising, or a whole other myriad of things. In contrast, they will have a sense of emptiness for all the years spent, keeping their hearts on the sidelines.

So again, I ask, what legacy, imprint, or impact do you want leave on the world? Where is your heart signaling you to go? I know, you don't know how to fully get there yet, but the how will work its way out. How deep is your heart's connection to the dream you wish to manifest? Are you ready to be joyful and have fun? Can you see where you are not in alignment in your life from these questions? Are you willing to look at nonlinear, nonsequential, and nontraditional solutions to get there? If you're having a tough time seeing it, ask someone near and dear to your heart how they see you. Sometimes, we've ignored our hearts for so long, we are not sure what alignment even looks in our lives. Just remember, now is the time to put your energy, your heart, and your deep love for yourself behind your actions and step out of the void.

CHAPTER 5

*"Man's ideal state is realized when
he has fulfilled the purpose for which
he is born. And what is it that reason
demands of him? Something very easy—
that he live in accordance
with his own nature."*

—SENECA

WELL, NOW I'VE shared the 4 Spiritual Laws of Money:

- ♡ Manifestation begins with desire.
- ♡ The heart is stronger than the brain.
- ♡ Intention redirects energy.
- ♡ The universe responds to action.

All four of these laws can be summed up in a single sentence: You, yes you, create your own life. Your outer life reflects what resides inside of you by your spoken words, thoughts, and feelings. These things produce the outcomes you have experienced. All of it! The more you use the words, thoughts, and feelings from a place of intentionality that aligns with your desires instead of your reactivity, the more you create a life that you will love. In other words, your outside life is a reflection of your inner world. Change the inside, and the outside will reflect something different back to you. Remember, you are the Creator. This means that to find what you are seeking on your journey is to walk the heart-centered talk. To align with heart-based conscious living gives you the result of deep, soulful happiness, joy, and contentment. The solution? Shift what's going on in the inside, which creates your outside life and how things show up outside of your-self, and everything falls right into place. This is why it's so important to show up in the world authentically.

If you choose to be a creator who lives in fear, life will be more stressful and full of struggle and you will not show up the way you want. If you fear something, like your significant other is going to leave, lo and behold, they do. The energy of your fear created that outcome. You were so focused on it that you pounced every time something supported that outcome until you made it happen. If you put out anxiety, fear, anger, drama, and negativity, it will all come back to you. Remember the Law of Attraction, which says that whatever energy you put into the grid comes back? Put happiness, gratitude, love, and joy out into the grid instead, and let the goodness boomerang. It feels way better. I know. I've lived it. The old saying is to treat people the way you wish to be treated; that includes treating yourself with kindness, love, and positivity, even if doing so disappoints everyone else in your life. Why? Because you matter too, along with everyone else.

When you work with the first Spiritual Law—**manifestation begins with desire**—you drop into your heart center and figure out where you want to go. Once you choose this alignment, the gateway just keeps opening up. This law is where you (re)discover the desire you wish to manifest to create real wealth. You don't let yourself or others put any limits on what you want to create. You change your vibration by allowing your heart center to take control of your life's path.

By using the Law of Attraction, you are manifesting your dreams using positive thought and affirmation. You are also invoking the Law of Manifestation to give birth to your dreams. Successful management of this law has you seeing with a crystal-clear vision from where you are today of what you desire to manifest; it also gives you the powerful belief and knowledge that you can do it and be flexible enough to allow that vision to expand as you build this manifestation muscle.

In the second law, **the heart is stronger than the brain**, you see that your heart should not only be considered in the process but the human heart is meant to be the leader of your life. Start with your heart, and then add your smarts! This spiritual truth requires you to not only find your center but to align with it as well by finding your soul's purpose and path. Follow your giggle, beat your own drum, and only do what makes you happy. This law doesn't say that your brain won't have input into your life's decisions; it just means that the brain won't be the leader or the loudest voice in the decision-making process of your life. You have to accept yourself and own your truth and allow yourself to live it. This knowing, accepting, and allowing puts you in a place of your true power. It gives you a strong core to build from in the rest of your life. This knowing, acceptance, and allowance also frees up more energy to manifest your dreams. Think about all the places in your life that you're not following your knowing and not accepting and allowing the flow of life and all the energy that goes into that resistance. If you free that energy up, imagine the amazing impact you will have not only on yourself but on all of those you impact in the energy grid around you. It's incredible to even think about it. Feel your way into that feeling of all that energy going into the positive. Wow, what a world we will live in when the majority of people surrender into this intentional direction of energy!

You have a place in the energy grid of the world, we all do, so take care of yourself. Look at yourself now, not in the muddy water of your past. It is a waste of energy to look back at what we cannot change. The keys to being successful with this law are to reduce your debt, eat high vibrational foods, give gratitude and love to others, share your happiness, and

live in your heart center. This raises your energy and makes room for your full potential.

Your heart and the things that make you happy raise the energy of the grid for everyone. Following your heart streamlines your path, and the opportunities that come along will help melt the obstacles away. Focus on the creation of the new, not the obstacles that created your current reality or the reality of the world around you. Be aware of your triggers and when you run across one, drop into your heart center to manage and resolve it. Remember, an emotional trigger means something inside of you needs to shift. It's not about the messenger that brought you the mirror; it is for you to do the work inside of you even though another person triggered the event. The reflection is a clear view of you.

Let your heart lead the way. It's okay to be vulnerable. The heart is the catalyst to align to why you are here. You want to be on your soul's path, otherwise you will continue to manifest crises that will force you off the path. I see it all the time; the further away you are from your path, the bigger the crisis you will call in, like a disease, accident, job layoff, etc. These happen to get you back on track. It's not that you should ignore your head, but you should allow your heart to lead the way. Remember, it's an "and" not an "or." You can follow your heart *and* provide for you, your family, and other loved ones. Often, we think that the money doesn't follow if we do follow our heart, yet nothing could be further from the truth. Use your mind to find the best way to fulfill your heart and soul's desires. Stay empowered by coming from a grounded, heart-centered place. Show up in the world in your truth with authenticity, gratitude, and love.

When you show up in the world how other people want you to, you are making their heart or head temporarily happy and not your own. Your life is not yours, it's theirs. This shows that your childhood rejection or trauma is still leading you and your old patterns are still affecting you. If you disappoint someone when you don't conform to their or a particular group's level of thinking or pressuring, it's okay to stand in your own power, as awkward as it may be. Their disappointment is not your responsibility. Remember, your job is to make yourself happy and empowered and it is their job to do the same. This is what raises the grid for all of us to our highest potential, individually and collectively. Standing your ground puts you in a place of abundance and prosperity with a deep knowing, in your gut, that all will be well. Then, and only then, will the money show up and stay in your life, because money is the result of standing in your truth and living it.

The third Spiritual Law of Money, **intention redirects energy**, shows us that where our focus goes, our creative and innovative energy will flow. When you are resolved to make your heart-centered visions into reality, your creator energy goes toward opening opportunities to make that happen. The path to success is to set the intention and find the courage to change. To implement the change, you must come from a place of personal empowerment and direct your energy potential to manifest your heart's desires. Raise your vibration with a new and different perception while breaking out of old patterns, others' expectations, and your past conditioning, and live life on your terms. Open up your eyes to all of your choices, intentions, and opportunities. Remember the Law of Attraction and keep your words, thoughts, and feelings positive and high vibrational. A pure sign that you are doing this successfully? You giggle and laugh often. Align your intentions with your heart to make the most of your creator energy.

The final law, **the universe responds to action**, encourages you to take steps toward your dream, to walk across that bridge of life—you can do it! Your dreams are just that—dreams that are up in the ethers of life until you choose to pull them down and do something about them. Participate in the creation of them. Bring those dreams into manifest form. Just take that one step in the right direction of your heart. Taking action cracks opportunities open; it shifts everything around you. Think of it like an egg; once you crack it, you can make an omelet, bake a cake, or pour it into a protein shake. You are off to the races with a whole new configuration. Right?! Can you see it? I know you can. Stop living from a place of fear and lack of vulnerability as if we have screen protectors for our lives. We don't have them, and there's a good reason why. It's totally okay to not have those protective shells. Allow yourself to crack open; you deserve it. Allow that energetic wall around your heart to dissolve. Allow yourself to fly to your highest potential in this lifetime! Often, taking these energetically walls down around your heart opens up so many opportunities that your intention and heart focus will be noticed. Remember, your heart is the strongest magnetic on this earth, so use it to your advantage. Open up that vulnerability. It's okay to be seen! It's your time!

This action step separates the successful from the Dreamers because without action, nothing happens. A body at rest stays at rest. One little push, and you are on your way. One little adjustment opens up opportunities. Even if you take a step in what is perceived to be the wrong direction, you have the right to correct your course and start again, but it helps you see life differently. That step in the wrong direction may show you that something you thought you were interested in was not really bound to make you happy. You've learned, and now you have more heart-based information because you are building that muscle to align your life in the most profound ways possible for you, and only you.

Successful use of this law means backing up your intentions with actions. Put your skin in the game of life to impact the world. Activate your life with your heartfelt energy. Take each step in the journey so that your manifestation can materialize in the physical. Do this by integrating your heart with your head and following your giggle, following that shit-eating grin you get for no apparent reason; you just deeply know you resonate with the flow at some profound level. It's a deep knowing that you are being you, all of you! Being in the flow means that time seems to stream forward, making our progress often seem effortless because we are following our hearts and time just flies by with this amazing alignment. Our journeys are so much faster once we are not struggling day to day and are living our soul's passion. It's like when a surfer catches a wave; just hang on for the ride of your life. It's truly amazing!

Using these Spiritual Laws, you not only awaken your wealth but also awaken your health, have better and more loving relationships, become passionate about your work/career again, and take a deep dive into your spiritual life by engaging in heart-based conscious living. This is the embodiment of *real wealth* in every facet of your life. This is not a one and done process because you can use these laws over and over wherever you are in your life. Each time, the result is a deeper understanding of self of what creates even more joy and happiness.

So, what is your heart's desire in your relationships? What would you love to manifest for your family life? What do you desire financially? When you approach life from your heart center, you have the advantage of knowing that you embody real wealth. The money always follows, and your financials will always be supported when you follow your soul's path. It is built on a solid foundation for sustainability. You won't be building up all this money at the cost of your soul so that half the money ends up going out the door from a divorce or some other catastrophe. At your work, you won't be slogging for a paycheck and wishing every day away until you can retire in five years, when they hand you a severance package. Living your life from your heart center allows you to impact all the areas of your life.

The best example of one following their soul's path is my mom. When she gave birth to the twelfth baby in my family, she stayed at my grandmas for a little while. One of my grandmother's neighbors came down to see her and the newborn, recalling a story of Mary (my mom) skipping down the block as a young girl, saying she was going to have twelve kids one day. The neighbor wanted to see the manifestation of my mom's life dream. Today, my mom is the mother of Marianne, Julie, Donnie, Brian, Matt, Colleen, Danny, Mark, Timmy, Peter, Johnny, and Katie . . . all twelve!

It's not logical for such a young woman at the age of five to say she wants to have twelve kids. It was an inside calling of my mother's heart that she followed through on. My dad was an electrician, and my mom was a stay-at-home parent. Through the years, they didn't have enough money to raise twelve kids. But as my mom was following her soul's path, things would just show up randomly when we needed them. Once, we found $5,000 in an envelope in our mailbox. One Christmas, when my mom had no idea how she was going to provide Christmas presents for twelve children, another family of thirteen wanted to adopt a family for Christmas. The thirteen children, who were all adults, gave presents to us. These things happen when you align your heart and mind to follow your soul's path. Again, it's not logical. It takes a lot of trust in your internal knowing, faith in who you are meant to be, and the courage to follow through with following your inner knowing all along the way!

When that twelfth child got to be in fourth grade, my mom got a bit crabby until, in her fifties, she went back to work to teach preschool kids. Once she was working with young children again, she was happy and healthy because again she was following her soul's path. And every time a new grandbaby is born, she just loves rocking them until the next one comes along... to date, she has thirty-eight grandkids and one more on the way.

Real wealth is more than just money. It is your heart aligned with your soul, your brain, and your gut. That alignment energizes your life and gives you infinite possibilities to get to your highest potential. It is not measured in dollars and cents. It is measured in giggles and leaps and bounds forward on your soul's path which results in financial wealth, great health and amazing relationships, personally and professionally. Real wealth is making your impact—the imprint and legacy you want to leave on this world—a reality.

What is your soul's path? What is your gift to the world? Raising kids? Being a CEO? Teaching? Writing? Programming? Cooking? It's time to follow that path. Give yourself permission to take that leap to a life you love. The path you follow is your choice, no one else's. Know that the minute you decide to take the leap to follow your heart, your life will start to align and support you. It is up to you to hold your power and energy so that you can empower the potential to let your heart make your choices. Every decision gets filtered through your heart first and foremost. You can set your intentions to follow your heart's desire instead of trudging on the treadmill of life. It's time to get out of the rat race many of us call life. Are you ready to have some fun, find your freedom, and raise the energy grid for everyone else at the same time? Remember, you are a **Creator**!

I am going to leave you with this final quote:

"Every great dream begins with a dreamer.
Always remember, you have within you
the strength, the patience, and the passion
to reach for the stars to change the world."

—HARRIET TUBMAN

EPILOGUE

WELCOME TO THE rest of your life!

This book brings a whole new awareness to what affects your ability to manifest your financial flow, from your income and expenses to your assets.

It's about approaching your finances from a place of empowerment, void of any fear. When coming from a place of empowerment, you are choosing a sustainable fuel source to create long-lasting happiness and joy. It's a state of power and grace that nothing else can replace. You'll have this deep knowing that, as you show up in the world in full alignment with why you are here, you're ready to plug into the rest of your life.

The key ingredient is the human heart. Why? The magnetic force of the human heart measures over eight miles. Your heart is the cornerstone to making all your dreams come true. You just need to learn how to use your internal electrical system to its greatest potential. To create a quantum leap in our lives, we must align with the vibration of the earth, nature, and others. None of this can happen unless we choose to connect to our own spirit, our own intuition, and our own knowing and have that be the beacon for our life's direction.

Remember, it's like building a muscle. Be patient and kind with yourself. You're learning a whole new way to plug into the world. You'll experience a lot of sobering moments as you realize and start to see that how you've shown up in your past hasn't served your highest good as you may have once thought. Every moment is as it should be, your soul knows it. Those moments are the building blocks to get you to exactly where you are today, ready for that quantum leap.

You've helped everyone else, now it's time to help yourself. As you begin to put your oxygen mask on first, putting your heart's dreams and desires as the foundation of every decision you make financially, personally, physically, mentally, emotionally, and spiritually, the progression of your life will flow uniquely. You'll wonder why you haven't realized this before. You'll consider why you went about it the hard way so many times.

You may find that the things, jobs, houses, vacations, friends, and other parts of your life no longer fit. That's because when you made those prior decisions, you didn't fully filter them through your heart. Parts were missing because your heart was fragmented when you made those choices. Forgive yourself for not knowing a more efficient way. Hold a state of grace for yourself as you are learning this new chapter to integrate it into your new life. Promise yourself that you will give yourself permission to expand, to grow, and have fun all along the way.

As you grieve all the time and energy spent climbing the career ladder, fighting for relationships that no longer serve the life you are meant to live, friendships that fall away because they are no longer a vibratory match, and all the other changes that will come your way, focus on your dreams and desires. Think the thoughts, speak the words, and feel the feelings of a life lived in your new alignment with your heart. Feel the joy and excitement as if you are already there.

Your life is what you choose to create! Now, take the bull by the horns and direct your life, your way.

From a practical level, understand your why behind every financial decision. How do the products and decisions you have or made support the dream, if they even do, now that you have redesigned the game plan?

Surround yourself with people who support your shifting and changing. Allow us to support you. Go to www.juliemurphy.com, and join our community to get the support you need as you are building the muscle of your new life. You don't have to do this on your own. We've got your back. We will walk all along the way right by your side.

Abundance is not just about money. It's about embodying real wealth. Be wealthy in all areas of your life; financially, physically, emotionally, mentally, and spiritually through your work in the world professionally and personally.

Trust your own timing. How things will unfold for you will not be in sync with anyone else because you are unique. You are special and have unique gifts to share with the world, and it's time to do so. Remember, we either work things out or act them out through our money, our health, and our relationships. It's time to rise above acting out in an unconscious manner and get busy living our purpose and passion.

Whether you are considered poor, a Debtor, a Dreamer, an Accumulator, or rich but empty, each and every one of you can embody real wealth at any age, at any time, and at any level of income and/or net worth. You just need to choose to get out of the push energy, out of the rat race of life, and live in the present moment, live in the now through your heart. The present moment is all you have, and it's time to fully be you, authentically you, in every way possible, and watch how all aligns in a more efficient way—efficiently bringing more money and more love with a deep feeling of being enough, being worthy, and certainly feeling loved in the greatest ways you have never imagined. Why? Because you are finally enough for yourself. You finally decided that you are worthy no matter what anyone else says, and you finally love yourself the way you've always deserved to feel loved. Once you do this, where you feel enough, worthy, and loved, then others

can show up the way you've always desired them to show up for you. They never could until you made yourself whole on the inside.

You have arrived! Now, let's pivot your life, resulting in a profound sense of freedom like no other.

Much love,
Julie

ACKNOWLEDGMENTS

WOW, WHERE TO start!

In my life, I've come to appreciate people that "Julie in her twenties" wouldn't have appreciated. Today, a wiser version of me absolutely appreciates all the souls that have played their part to get the real Julie, the authentic Julie, at her core, out of the closet.

Billy Rapka, fellow adventurist, twin flame, business partner, lover, and catalyst to open my heart wide open again, I am eternally grateful for our journey together! Thank you for your help getting this book into manifest form. I appreciate you holding me accountable and nudging me into the best version of myself and loving me all along the way. From the deepest part of my heart, thank you for sharing your heart to bring this book and work out to the world!

Mark Murphy, my little brother and business partner, thank you for holding the container for our wealth management business while I push the limits on the industry to bring the human heart back into our world of finance. This book would not have been possible if you didn't create the space for me to take time to manifest it into the world.

To all my mentors, teachers, and coaches, you know I love you with all of my heart. Thanks for helping me chip away from my own trauma patterns that landed in my subconscious mind from my childhood. Thank you for helping me evolve into the best version of me so I could bring this work into the world. Thank you, David Gilardy, Panache Desai, Anne Emerson, Deirdre Morgan, Bob Lyman, Karyn Pettigrew, Marie-France Collin, Leo Cordero and his team, Justin Nahum Vizakis, Aaron Doughty, Victor and Pattie Otto, and Rita Hickman.

Thank you to my support team that helped me bring this book into manifest form. Lisa Schell and Laura Yates, when I wanted to be one big run-on sentence, I'm grateful for your gifts of editing and your abilities to interpret the words written from the heart. You have amazing talent. Thank you for sharing your gifts.

To all that is and ever shall be . . .

ABOUT THE AUTHOR

 JULIE MARIE MURPHY, CLU, ChFC, MBA, CFP®, has more than 27 years' experience as a CERTIFIED FINANCIAL PLANNER™ and is often referred to as a *financial healer* or *money therapist*. She is turning the personal finance industry upside down by redefining standard financial planning approaches and educating people about a new way of finding financial success, *following a process which starts from within* to embody a life of real wealth!

Julie's first book, *The Emotion Behind Money: Building Wealth from the Inside Out*, focused on really recognizing how emotions are entangled in our financial world and how to work through them in a healthy manner.

Her second book, *Awaken Your Wealth: Creating a PACT to Optimize Your Money and Your Life*, reached #1 in multiple categories on Amazon. A reader review stated, "If Warren Buffet and Ghandi wrote a book together it would result in something like this."

Julie has helped at large, being seen on WGN Chicago, CNBC-TV, Lifetime TV, Oprah & Friends Radio, The Wall Street Journal, Associated Press, and more. Julie is the founder of JMC Wealth Management, Inc., in Chicago. She is also a motivational speaker, media expert, podcaster expert on the topic of emotions and money and holistic financial and life planning.

www.jmcwealth.com
www.juliemurphy.com